BY SIMON AND ALISON HOLST

Published by
Hyndman Publishing
325 Purchas Road, RD2
Amberley 7482
ISBN 1-877168-03-3

© TEXT: Simon & Alison Holst
DESIGNER: Rob Di Leva
PHOTOGRAPHER: Lindsay Keats
PROPS: Gaye Bergquist
HOME ECONOMISTS: Simon &
Alison Holst, Jane Ritchie,
Dee Harris
PRINTING: Spectrum Print

The recipes in this book have been carefully
tested by the authors. The publisher and the
authors have made every effort to ensure that the
instructions are accurate and safe, but they
cannot accept liability for any resulting injury or
loss or damage to property whether direct or
consequential.

Because ovens and microwave ovens vary so
much, you should use the cooking times
suggested in recipes as guides only. The first time
you make a recipe, check it at intervals to make
sure it is not cooking faster, or more slowly than
expected.

Always follow the detailed instructions given by
the manufacturers of your appliances and
equipment, rather than the more general
instructions given in these recipes.

About this book

What could be more welcoming than the wonderful aroma of fresh, homemade bread!

Bread is very definitely a rising star in the food world! Why? Not just because interesting bread tastes great, but because the humble loaf is GOOD for us too, high in complex carbohydrates and low in fat. You will be doing hungry children a good turn when you encourage them to eat more bread, with, and in between meals.

When you make bread, you use only a few inexpensive ingredients — and your skill — to turn the simplest meal into something which your guests will find truly memorable!

If you are a breadmaking novice, I hope that you will start with a basic bread or two, then try many other recipes once you have "got the feel" of this satisfying yeast cookery.

In this book, we are not suggesting that making bread with a bread machine is better than making it by hand — or vice versa. Both methods have their advantages! I must admit that I expected to find that machine-made breads were not as good as their handmade counterparts, and I was taken aback to find that this was certainly not the case on many occasions. I was quite overwhelmed as Simon produced loaf after loaf of new and exciting high quality breads from the machines with which he was working.

What had I been doing wrong all these years? Why had my hand-made breads not looked and tasted like these loaves? Part of the answer lay in the ingredients. The right flour, the correct yeast and some extra ingredients which I had not previously used certainly made a difference, producing fine-

Contents

textured, nicely risen breads which seemed almost as good the next day, and sometimes even a couple of days later. Simon's experience and interest in bread after working as a food scientist in a bread laboratory for several years undoubtedly helped too!

As Jane Ritchie and I donned white aprons and mixed and kneaded at length, with the microwave tinging, the dough hook turning, and timers buzzing all over the place, breads of similar quality, of varied shapes and sizes emerged from my oven too. What fun! How satisfying!

Simon and I hope that you will get a great deal of pleasure from the breads you make, as you fill your home with wonderful yeasty aromas, and delight those around your table.

Making bread with a bread machine

We think that bread machines are truly wonderful - almost too good to be true!

Fancy being able to measure a few basic ingredients into a machine, then pressing two or three buttons, and coming back a few hours later (or waking up in the morning) to remove a warm, fragrant, ready-to-eat loaf of bread!

This however, is only part of the story. Through this book you will see photos of our breads. Some were made as above, while others were mixed, kneaded and risen in a bread machine, then taken out, shaped by hand, and baked in a regular oven.

To our way of thinking, the machine did all the rather messy and tedious work, leaving us the fun part, hand-shaping warm, satiny dough. When you use a bread machine in this way, you greatly increase the range and type of breads you can make. What's more, you don't think twice about making breads like pizzas and pita breads which your family eats often.

People keep asking us if bread machines are worth the initial investment. We think they are, as long as you use them regularly, and especially if you make hand-shaped and fancy breads which cost much more than regular basic loaves to buy. For example, when you make a dozen or so croissants or bagels, you may save over $15 per batch.

There are a number of bread machines on the market. Most are designed to make loaves which weigh around 750g. Our recipes are written for these, and use about 3 cups of flour. If you have a smaller machine, with a book of recipes which use about 2 cups of flour, you can scale down our recipes, using the table on the last page. If your machine is bigger than the ones we used, you can scale the recipes up, or use them as they are.

The manufacturers of different machines suggest adding ingredients in different orders. Always follow their guidelines, especially if you are using the timer setting.

Some machines work best with slightly different liquid to flour ratios. Whenever you try a new recipe, be prepared to experiment a little, and make small changes if necessary. **We find that the best way to ensure success is to always check the dough in its first few minutes of kneading.** It is fun to watch the machine getting under way, anyway! Don't be afraid to open the machine to do this. Within 5 minutes, the dough should have formed an even, round ball or cylinder that is not too sticky. If it looks too dry, add 1 -2 tablespoons of water gradually. If it is too wet, add 1-2 tablespoons of flour. You will quickly learn what dough consistency gives the best results in your machine.

From time to time, you may find that you have trouble with your "tried and true" recipes. Don't be alarmed, read the book that came with your bread machine, and the suggestions on page 6, and try again. Remember that bread dough is really a living thing, and its behaviour may be affected by many factors.

Making bread by hand

Like many other people, we get a great deal of pleasure and satisfaction from making bread by hand.

Once you get into a bread-making routine, you will wonder why you ever considered it a complicated procedure. Although the whole process involves a number of steps, few of these are very time-consuming, and they may be fitted in between many other activities.

It is good to think that, using your breadmaking skills, you can start with a few basic, inexpensive ingredients, and some very simple equipment, and finish up with spectacularly good breads, literally made with your own hands, of which you can be justifiably proud.

As you become an experienced bread-maker, you will "get the feel of" the dough, adding flour, and often other ingredients as necessary, rather than in fixed amounts, and using the amounts given in the recipe as a guide only. We are sure that once you know what you are doing, you will start changing our recipes, and developing your own specialties.

Don't try to produce bread which is identical with commercially made, light textured, white sandwich bread, and don't expect your homemade breads to stay fresh for a week! Enjoy instead, the many unique breads you can make using interesting and different ingredients, and enjoy them hot from the oven, or at least within a couple of days.

After making all the recipes in this book by hand, often several times, we decided there were several pieces of equipment which were invaluable.

First of these is a timer - there is nothing worse than forgetting when your bread is ready for its next step!

Because the first few minutes of kneading a soft dough can be messy, we like a straight-sided plastic scraper to lift off the pieces of dough which stick to our work surface.

We think that a sturdy food mixer with a dough hook is a great help to anyone who makes handmade bread regularly, although we know that some bread-makers will not agree with us! A dough hook will knead a dough which is softer than you can knead by hand, freeing you for 10 minutes to clean up and do other things.

One of the reasons bread machines make such good bread is that the process is timed and cannot be speeded up by impatient cooks. If you "shortcut" and hurry from one breadmaking step to the next you are likely to have disappointing results.

The two most important processes are kneading and rising (see page 7). If you have a friend who makes bread, watch her or him kneading (since actions are better than words) then try, yourself. Our instructions give fairly specific rising times. These relate to good conditions (see page 7).

Although we know that you will be eager to eat your bread as soon as possible, remember that it will cut much better if you leave it for an hour or so, to cool down. A really sharp bread knife is really worthwhile (see page 64).

We hope that you will have fun making, sharing and eating our breads.

Bread Machine Tips

First, an important message from Alison! However excited you may be about the wonderful things a new machine will do, you may be daunted by the idea of "getting the thing going!"

Since my children were 10–12 years old, I have found that the best way to learn about a new machine is to encourage them to read the instructions and use the machine. I then get them to show me what to do, and operate it under their supervision, preferably several times. After this, I am "away laughing", can now read the instruction book and understand it, and can see just how simple the machine is.

If you are not completely familiar with your bread machine, you might try the same thing, borrowing a neighbour's child if necessary!

After these first steps, we hope that you will read all the pages in this book which do NOT contain recipes, because they are written to help you! Read the booklets which come with your bread machine every few weeks — or whenever you have teething problems — because you are sure to learn some finer points each time. The manufacturer knows your particular machine better than we do, but these are answers we have found by trial and error.

Sunken top and/or collapsed middle?
Too much water — try 2 tablespoons less
Too much yeast — try ½ teaspoon less (the dough rises too quickly, then collapses before baking)
No salt, or too little salt (salt slows down yeast and "tightens" the dough)
The room temperature/humidity is too high — try a quick cycle

Coarse or holey texture?
Too much liquid — try 2 tablespoons less
Fermenting too quickly, try a short cycle
Room temperature too high
Too much sugar — use ½ teaspoon less

Uneven top?
Dough too stiff, not enough water — try adding 1–2 tablespoons

Small compact loaf or poor rising?
Too little yeast
No yeast. Did you forget it?
Yeast beyond expiry date
Measurement errors — not enough yeast or water, or too much salt
Dough too stiff — not enough water
Yeast has reacted with water too soon when using time delay - check the order in which ingredients should be added. If you are using the rapid cycle, try adding an extra ½ teaspoon of yeast and another teaspoon of sugar.

We found that it was much easier to put ingredients in the bread machine bowl if we took the bowl out of the machine first.

Kneading and Rising

KNEADING: The best way to learn to knead bread is to watch an experienced bread-maker kneading dough from the stage where it is turned out of its mixing bowl, until it is smooth and satiny, does not stick to the working surface, and springs back when pressed with a finger.

To keep the dough as soft as possible, add no more flour than necessary, but use enough to stop it sticking to your hands and the bench. Our way of kneading is to push the dough down firmly, away from us, using the "heel" of one hand, then collect it with a circular movement of the other hand, bringing it back to the position where it can be pushed away again. The dough should travel more or less in a circle.

The dough hook of a strong electric mixer will knead bread dough efficiently, too. Dough hooks save time and energy if you make handmade bread regularly.

However you knead your dough, count the minutes spent, since sufficient time and work is required to change the structure of the dough.

RISING DOUGH: Bread dough "rises" or increases in volume because it contains yeast which grows and multiplies, producing bubbles of carbon dioxide which are trapped in the kneaded dough.

Yeast grows best when warm. When cold, it grows very slowly. If it gets too hot it is killed, and the dough will never rise.

A place of just the right warmth is therefore very important.

To keep a pocket of still, warm air, above the yeast mixture while it is rising, we cover the bowl of dough.

We find that the most reliable and successful places to rise our doughs and loaves are our microwave ovens and the conventional ovens in which we will later bake our breads.

Microwave the covered glass or plastic bowl of dough on Defrost, 30% power, for 1 minute, at 5–10 minute intervals. Always check the dough temperature before you microwave it again.

To warm conventional ovens for rising bread, heat a gas oven for one minute, and an electric oven for 2–3 minutes, at intervals. Check for warmth by putting your hand in the oven. ALWAYS remove the dough while heating either oven, so your bread cannot overheat if you are called away or have a memory lapse!

After the risen bread is put in the oven to bake, it expands still further. We have found that it often expands more if it is baked without the fan on for the first 15 minutes.

Our Favourite White Bread

We find it enormously satisfying to make this delicious, sweet-smelling, finely textured, nicely risen white loaf.
Add a little butter, and some homemade raspberry jam or honey and you have food for the gods!

Makes a large loaf (7–8 cup pan):

3 tsp Surebake yeast
1¼ cups plus 2 Tbsp warm water
2 Tbsp lecithin granules or oil
2 tsp sugar
1½ tsp salt
2 Tbsp non-fat milk powder
3 cups Champion High Grade Flour

Bread Machine Instructions

Carefully measure all the ingredients into a 750g capacity bread machine, in the order specified by the manufacturer.

Set to the NORMAL/WHITE bread cycle, MEDIUM crust and START (or use the DOUGH cycle and shape and bake by hand). This is a very good timer bread.

Handmade Bread Instructions

Measure the first six ingredients into a large bowl. Add 1½ cups of the measured high grade flour and mix thoroughly. Cover and leave for 15 minutes or longer in a warm place.

Stir in the remaining flour, adding a little extra warm water or high grade flour if necessary, to make a dough just firm enough to knead.

Knead with the dough hook of an electric mixer or by hand on a lightly floured surface for 10 minutes, adding extra flour if necessary, until the dough forms a soft ball which springs back when pressed gently.

Turn the dough in 2–3 teaspoons of oil in the cleaned, dry bowl, cover with cling film and leave in a warm draught-free place for about 30 minutes.

Knead the oiled dough lightly in the bowl for a minute, then pat it into a square a little longer than the baking pan. Roll dough into a cylinder, then put into the sprayed or buttered bread pan, pressing it into the corners and levelling the top.

Leave to rise, in a warm, draught-free place for about an hour, or until double its original size.

If desired, brush with milk or egg glaze (page 59) and sprinkle with sesame seeds, then bake at 200°C for about 30 minutes or until the unmoulded loaf has a browned bottom and sides and sounds hollow when tapped.

Wholemeal Bread

This recipe gives a good sized loaf of traditional "brown" bread. Not only is it delicious, with the light texture children love, but it is also an excellent source of fibre. Use it for good hearty sandwiches or toast.

Makes a medium loaf (6 – 8 cup pan):

3 tsp Surebake yeast
1½ cups warm water
2 tsp sugar
1 tsp salt
2 Tbsp lecithin granules or oil   Consder
2 Tbsp gluten flour
2 Tbsp non-fat milk powder, optional
3 cups Champion Wholemeal Flour
2 Tbsp wheatgerm, optional

Bread Machine Instructions

Carefully measure all the ingredients into a 750g capacity bread machine, in the order specified by the manufacturer.

Set to the NORMAL/WHITE or WHOLE WHEAT cycle, MEDIUM crust and START. This is a good timer bread.

Handmade Bread Instructions

Measure the first six ingredients (plus milk powder, if using) into a large bowl, add 1½ cups of the wholemeal flour and mix thoroughly. Cover and leave for 15 minutes or longer in a warm place.

Stir in the remaining wholemeal flour and optional wheatgerm, add a little extra flour if necessary to make a dough just firm enough to knead.

Knead with the dough hook of an electric mixer or by hand on a lightly floured surface for 10 minutes, adding extra flour if necessary, until the dough forms a soft ball which springs back when pressed gently.

Turn in 2–3 teaspoons of oil in the cleaned, dry bowl, cover with cling film and leave in a warm draught-free place for 30–40 minutes.

Knead the dough lightly in the bowl for a minute, then pat it into a square a little longer than the loaf pan. Roll the dough into a cylinder and place it in the sprayed or buttered pan, pressing it into the corners and levelling the top.

Leave to rise in a warm, draught-free place for about an hour, or until double the original size.

Bake at 200°C for about 30 minutes or until the unmoulded loaf has a browned bottom and sides and sounds hollow when tapped.

Notes:—
Done on 17.1.01

Cheese Muffin Bread

Bake this as a rich cheese loaf, top with grated cheese and cook like muffins in pans, or make novel pull-apart Monkey breads if you feel like something different.

Makes a large loaf, 12 muffin buns, or two 18cm rings of "Monkey bread":

3 tsp Surebake yeast
¾ cup warm water
2 large eggs
2 Tbsp lecithin granules or butter
2 tsp sugar
1 tsp salt
2 Tbsp non-fat milk powder
3 cups Champion High Grade Flour
¾ cup grated tasty cheese
½ tsp chili powder, optional
melted butter
grated Parmesan or tasty cheese

Bread Machine Instructions

Carefully measure the first eight ingredients into a 750g capacity bread machine, in the order specified by the manufacturer. Set to the NORMAL/WHITE bread cycle, MEDIUM crust and START (or use the dough cycle and shape and bake using the instructions given below).

Handmade Bread Instructions

Measure the first seven ingredients into a large bowl with 1½ cups of high grade flour and mix thoroughly. Cover and leave for 15 minutes or longer in a warm place.

Stir in the remaining flour, the cheese and chili powder and a little extra flour or water if necessary to make a dough just firm enough to knead.

Knead with the dough hook of an electric mixer or by hand on a lightly floured surface for 10 minutes, adding extra flour if necessary, until the dough forms a soft ball which springs back when lightly pressed.

Turn the dough in 2–3 teaspoons of oil in the cleaned, dry bowl, cover with cling film and leave in a warm draught-free place for 30–40 minutes.

Knead the dough lightly in the bowl for a minute, then shape as desired.

To make a loaf: Shape as on page 8.

To make Muffin Buns: Divide the dough into 12 pieces and roll into balls. Place in sprayed medium-size muffin pans and leave to rise in a warm draught-free place for 1 hour, or until doubled in volume. Dampen tops with milk and sprinkle with grated tasty cheese. Bake at 220°C for 10–12 minutes until tops, sides and bottom are golden brown.

To make "Monkey Bread": Divide the dough into four, then eight, then 16, then 32 more-or-less equal sized pieces. Roll each ball in a little melted butter then in grated Parmesan or tasty cheese. Line the bottom of two 20cm ring pans with baking paper and oil the sides. Place 16 of the cheesy balls of dough evenly around each tin. Cover with cling film and leave to rise in a warm draught-free place for about an hour or until almost double in volume. Bake at 220°C for 15–20 minutes or until golden brown. Serve warm.

Mixed Grain Bread

Pre-cooking the kibbled grains may seem a bit fiddly, but it ensures a moist loaf. The large, light textured loaf, flecked with kibbled grains is a just reward for the extra effort!

Makes a large loaf (8 cup pan):

½ cup mixed kibbled grains*
1¼ cups cold water
3 tsp Surebake yeast
2 Tbsp olive oil
1 Tbsp sugar
1½ tsp salt
2 Tbsp lecithin granules, optional
1 cup Champion Wholemeal Flour
2½ cups Champion High Grade Flour

* Buy or make a mixture of kibbled wheat, red and/or purple wheat, and kibbled rye.

Prepare the kibble

In a small pot, cover the kibble mix with 2–3 cups of cold water. Bring to the boil, then simmer for 1–2 minutes. Take from the heat and drain well in a sieve.

Bread Machine Instructions

Carefully measure all the ingredients, including the prepared kibble combined with the measured water, into a 750g capacity bread machine, in the order specified by the manufacturer.

Set to the NORMAL/WHITE bread cycle, MEDIUM crust and START. This is a good timer bread.

Handmade Bread Instructions

In a large bowl, mix the prepared kibbled grains with the cold water listed. Add all remaining ingredients except the high grade flour. Mix thoroughly, cover and leave 15 minutes in a warm place.

Stir in the high grade flour, adding a little extra water or flour if necessary, to make a dough just firm enough to knead.

Knead with the dough hook of an electric mixer or by hand on a lightly floured surface for 10 minutes, adding extra flour if necessary, until the dough forms a soft ball which springs back when pressed gently.

Turn dough in 2–3 teaspoons of oil in the cleaned, dry bowl, cover with cling film and leave in a warm draught-free place for 30 minutes.

Knead the oiled dough lightly in the bowl for a minute, then pat into a square a little longer than the baking pan. Roll dough into a cylinder, then put into the buttered or sprayed bread pan, pressing it into the corners and levelling the top.

Leave to rise in a warm, draught-free place for about an hour, or until double its original size. If desired, brush with milk or egg glaze (page 59) and sprinkle with extra kibbled grains, then bake at 200°C for about 30 minutes, until the unmoulded loaf has a browned bottom and sides and sounds hollow when tapped.

Heavy Multigrain Bread

To get a flattish loaf like the dense multigrain breads you buy, you need a dough which is much wetter than normal bread dough.
As these loaves are very moist you may find it best to slice them the next day, or even the day after that!

Makes a large loaf (6 – 8 cup pan):

¾ cup mixed kibbled grains*

1¾ cups cold water (plus 1–2 Tbsp if required)

3 tsp Surebake yeast

2 tsp sugar

1½ tsp salt

1 Tbsp lecithin granules or butter

3 Tbsp non-fat milk powder

2 Tbsp gluten flour

3 cups Champion Wholemeal Flour

*Buy or make a mixture of kibbled wheat, red and/or purple wheat, and kibbled rye.

Prepare the kibble

Place the kibble mix in a pot and cover with cold water. Bring to the boil then remove from the heat. Allow to stand for a few minutes, then drain in a sieve.

Bread Machine Instructions

Carefully measure all the ingredients including the prepared kibble combined with the measured water into a 750g capacity bread machine, in the order specified by the manufacturer.

Try the NORMAL/WHITE bread cycle, MEDIUM crust setting, but you may find that you need to experiment with other settings to get the best results from your machine.

Check the dough after about 5 minutes of mixing — it should barely be holding its round shape. Add the extra water or a little more flour if required.

Handmade Bread Instructions

Prepare the kibble mix as in the instructions above. Put in a large bowl with the measured cold water and the remaining ingredients and mix thoroughly.

Knead with the dough hook of an electric mixer for about 10 minutes, then spread the wet mixture evenly in a well sprayed or buttered 6 – 8 cup loaf pan and leave it to rise in a warm draught-free place for 45–60 minutes, or until double its original size.

Bake at 180°C for 45–60 minutes or until a skewer inserted deeply in the centre of the loaf comes out clean, and until the unmoulded loaf sounds hollow when tapped on the bottom.

Note: Whether you are making this loaf in a bread machine or by hand, you may have to adjust the quantities of flour and water a little. (We have found this necessary when changing bags of flour). The mixture should be pourable and spreadable, with a consistency somewhere between a very soft dough and a batter. Leave for 24 hours before slicing.

Our Favourite White Bread, Heavy Multigrain Bread, hand & machine made.

Sundried Tomato, Herbed Parmesan and Dark Rye Breads.

Dark Rye Bread

This large loaf has a wonderfully rich, dark colour, an inviting aroma, interesting flavour, and is very popular.
You can vary the colour and flavour of the bread to suit your own taste.

Makes a large loaf weighing about 900g:

3 tsp Surebake yeast
1½ cups warm water
2 Tbsp golden syrup
2 Tbsp oil
1½ tsp salt
2 cups Champion High Grade Flour
1½ cups rye meal
2 Tbsp cocoa powder
1 tsp instant coffee granules
about 1 tsp caraway seeds

Bread Machine Instructions

Carefully measure all the ingredients into a 750g capacity bread machine, in the order specified by the manufacturer.

Set to the NORMAL/WHITE bread cycle, MEDIUM crust and START (or use DOUGH cycle and shape and bake as below). This is a good timer bread.

Handmade Bread Instructions

Measure the first five ingredients into a large bowl with 1 cup of high grade flour and mix thoroughly. Cover and leave to stand in a warm place for 15 minutes.

Stir in the remaining flour, the rye meal, cocoa powder, instant coffee and caraway seeds. Add a little extra flour or water to make a dough just firm enough to knead.

Knead with the dough hook of an electric mixer or by hand on a lightly floured surface for 10 minutes, adding extra flour if necessary, until the dough forms a soft ball which springs back when pressed lightly.

Turn in 2–3 teaspoons of oil in the cleaned, dry bowl, cover with cling film and leave in a warm draught-free place for 30 minutes.

Knead the dough lightly in the bowl for a

minute before turning out onto a lightly floured surface.

To make a round loaf, pat the dough into a ball, flatten this slightly with your hand, then pick it up and tuck and pinch all the edges underneath, so the top of the dough is smooth and stretched, and will form an evenly rounded loaf when baked.

To help keep its shape, place the round loaf in a 23cm round pan, (loose-bottomed if possible) and dust with flour. Leave in a warm draught-free place for about 1 hour or until risen to about twice its original size.

Bake at 200°C for about 30 minutes or until the unmoulded loaf sounds hollow when the bottom is tapped.

Variation: For a light rye loaf, leave out the cocoa powder and instant coffee. Vary the amount of caraway seed to suit your taste.

Sundried Tomato Bread

The tomato paste in this bread gives it a warm, "sunny" colour, and the sun-dried tomatoes give it a definite tomato flavour.
Serve it with a light pasta dish and/or salad to make a delicious summer meal.

Makes a large loaf (6–8 cup pan):

3 tsp Surebake yeast
1 cup warm water
¼ cup tomato paste
2 tsp sugar
1 tsp salt
2 Tbsp lecithin granules or oil
1 cup Champion Wholemeal Flour
2 cups Champion High Grade Flour
1 Tbsp chopped fresh basil, optional
¼ cup chopped sundried tomatoes

Bread Machine Instructions

Carefully measure all the ingredients into a 750g capacity bread machine, in the order specified by the manufacturer.

Set to the NORMAL/WHITE bread cycle, MEDIUM crust and START (or use the DOUGH cycle and shape by hand). This is a good timer bread.

Handmade Bread Instructions

Measure the first seven ingredients into a large bowl and mix thoroughly. Cover and leave for 15 minutes or longer in a warm place.

Stir in the high grade flour, basil and the sundried tomatoes, adding extra high grade flour if necessary, to make a soft dough, just firm enough to knead.

Knead with the dough hook of an electric mixer or by hand on a lightly floured surface for 10 minutes, until the dough forms a soft ball which springs back when pressed gently.

Turn dough in 2–3 teaspoons of oil in a cleaned, dry bowl, cover with cling film and leave in a warm draught-free place for about 30 minutes.

Knead the oiled dough lightly in the bowl for a minute. Turn it out onto a lightly floured surface, then pat it into a square a little longer than the baking pan. Roll the dough into a cylinder, then put it into the buttered or sprayed bread pan, pressing it into the corners and levelling the top.

Leave to rise in a warm draught-free place for about an hour, or until the dough has doubled in size.

If desired, brush with milk or egg glaze (page 59) and bake at 200°C for about 30 minutes or until the unmoulded loaf has browned on its bottom and sides and sounds hollow when tapped.

Variations: Spread basil pesto over the dough before you roll it up, so you see a dark green spiral in each cut slice, or shape the dough as for Focaccia (page 28) adding basil pesto and Parmesan cheese (or other) toppings.

Herbed Parmesan Bread

Serve this herby bread with a soup or salad to make a substantial light meal, or try brushing thick slices with garlic oil and grilling them for an interesting snack.

Makes a large loaf (8 cup pan):

3 tsp Surebake yeast

1¼ cups warm water

2 Tbsp lecithin granules or oil

2 tsp sugar

1 tsp salt

1 cup Champion Wholemeal Flour

2 cups Champion High Grade Flour

¼ cup grated Parmesan

¼ cup pesto

¼ cup finely chopped fresh herbs

Bread Machine Instructions

Carefully measure all the ingredients into a 750g capacity bread machine, in the order specified by the manufacturer.

Set to the NORMAL/WHITE bread cycle, MEDIUM crust and START (or use the DOUGH cycle and shape and bake as described below). This is a good timer bread.

Handmade Bread Instructions

Measure the first six ingredients into a large bowl and mix thoroughly. Cover and leave for 15 minutes or longer in a warm place.

Stir in the high grade flour, grated Parmesan, pesto and chopped herbs (if using) then stir to make a soft dough, just firm enough to knead, adding a little extra flour if necessary.

Knead with the dough hook of an electric mixer or by hand on a lightly floured surface for 10 minutes, adding extra flour if necessary, until the dough forms a soft ball and springs back when pressed gently.

Turn dough in 2–3 teaspoons of oil in the cleaned, dry bowl, cover with cling film and leave in a warm draught-free place for about 30 minutes.

Knead the oiled dough lightly in the bowl for a minute, then pat into a square a little longer than the baking pan. Roll dough into a cylinder, then put in the buttered or sprayed bread pan, pressing it into the corners and levelling the top.

Leave to rise in a warm draught-free place for about an hour, or until the dough has doubled in size.

Brush with milk or egg glaze (page 59) and bake at 200°C for 30 minutes or until the unmoulded loaf has a browned bottom and sides and sounds hollow when tapped.

Variations: Use dough to make Monkey Bread (page 10) or rolls (page 18).

Yoghurt Bread or Rolls

These chewy little rolls have a fine texture and an interesting, slightly sour flavour. They make good dinner rolls and freeze well, too. Consider making them when you do not have the time to make traditional sourdough rolls.

Makes a large loaf or 12 rolls:

3 tsp Surebake yeast

¾ cup plain, unsweetened yoghurt

½ cup warm water

2 Tbsp lecithin granules or oil

2 tsp sugar

1 tsp salt

3 cups Champion High Grade Flour

Bread Machine Instructions

Carefully measure all the ingredients into a 750g capacity bread machine, in the order specified by the manufacturer.

Set to the NORMAL/WHITE bread cycle, MEDIUM crust and START (or use the DOUGH cycle and shape and bake as described below). This is a good timer bread.

Note: The thickness of yoghurt varies, so check the dough after about 5 minutes of mixing and add a little extra water if it looks too dry.

Handmade Bread Instructions

Measure the first six ingredients into a large bowl with 1 cup of the flour and mix thoroughly. Cover and leave for 15 minutes or longer in a warm place. Add the rest of the flour and stir to make a soft dough, adding a little extra warm water or flour if necessary.

Knead with the dough hook of an electric mixer or by hand on a lightly floured surface for 10 minutes, adding extra water or flour if necessary, until dough is smooth and satiny, and springs back when pressed gently.

Turn dough in 1–2 teaspoons of oil in the cleaned dry bowl, cover with cling film and leave in a warm draught-free place for 30 minutes. Lightly knead the oiled dough in the bowl for a minute.

Shaping and Baking

Roll the dough into a single long loaf or cut into 12 equal pieces (each about 75 grams). Roll each piece into sausage shapes 12 cm long, or into round rolls. (For smooth-topped round rolls, make your thumb and forefinger in a ring shape and push a piece dough through the ring, so the dough on the top of the roll is stretched and the edges are pinched together underneath it.)

Place the long loaf diagonally on an oiled oven tray. Put the prepared rolls on two oiled oven trays, leaving room for them to spread.

Leave to rise in a warm draught-free place for about an hour, or until doubled in size/thickness. After half an hour slash the top/s of the rolls or loaf diagonally, with a very sharp knife.

Spray with water if you want a crusty outside, or brush with milk or egg glaze (page 59) then bake at 200°C until evenly browned top and bottom, about 15 minutes for the rolls or 20–25 minutes for a single long loaf.

Hamburger Buns and Hot Dog Rolls

These tasty white buns and rolls are just right for Hot Dogs and Hamburgers. The texture will be as popular with adults as it is with children — not too firm, but not too soft. Try them for your next barbecue.

For about 8 buns or rolls:

3 tsp Surebake yeast
1 cup warm water
50g butter
1 Tbsp sugar
1 tsp salt
2 Tbsp non-fat milk powder
3 cups Champion High Grade Flour

Bread Machine Instructions

Carefully measure all the ingredients into a 750g capacity bread machine, in the order specified by the manufacturer.

Set to the DOUGH cycle, and START.

When the cycle is complete, remove the dough from the machine and shape then bake them as below.

Handmade Bread Instructions

Measure the first six ingredients into a large bowl with $1\frac{1}{2}$ cups of the flour, and mix thoroughly. Cover and leave for 15 minutes or longer in a warm place.

Stir in the remaining flour, adding as much as you need to make a dough just firm enough to knead.

Knead with the dough hook of an electric mixer or by hand on a lightly floured surface for 10 minutes, adding extra flour if necessary, until the dough forms a soft ball which springs back when pressed gently.

Turn in 2–3 teaspoons of oil in the cleaned, dry bowl, cover with cling film and leave in a warm draught-free place for 30–40 minutes.

Knead the dough lightly in the bowl for a minute then turn out onto a lightly floured surface.

Shaping and Baking

Cut the dough into four, then eight pieces each about 100g.

To make Hamburger buns: Roll each piece into a smooth ball, then flatten into circles, about 9cms across.

To make Hot Dog buns: Roll each piece of dough into "cigar" shape, about 18cm long.

Arrange on oiled or well sprayed baking trays and leave to rise in a warm draught-free place for about an hour, or until the buns have approximately doubled in size.

Brush with egg glaze (page 59) and sprinkle with toasted sesame seeds if desired.

Bake at 200°C for 12-15 minutes until golden brown top and bottom.

Pizzas & Pita Breads

One of the real joys of a owning a breadmaker is how really easy it is to make good yeasty pizza bases!
Simply measure in the ingredients, set to the dough cycle and go away. The hardest part becomes selecting your toppings!

Makes 1 very large Pizza, 2 medium Pizzas or 8 medium Pita Breads:

2 tsp active dried yeast
1 cup plus 2 Tbsp warm water
2 tsp sugar
1 tsp salt
2 Tbsp olive oil
3 cups Champion High Grade Flour

Bread Machine Instructions

Carefully measure all the ingredients into a 750g capacity bread machine, in the order specified by the manufacturer.

Set to DOUGH cycle and START. When the cycle is complete, take the dough out of the machine and shape and bake it as below.

Handmade Bread Instructions

Measure the first five ingredients into a large bowl with 1 cup of the measured flour and mix thoroughly. Cover and leave for 15 minutes, or longer in a warm place. Stir in the remaining flour, adding extra if necessary, to make a dough just firm enough to knead.

Knead with the dough hook of an electric mixer or by hand on a lightly floured surface for 10 minutes, adding extra flour if necessary, until the dough forms a soft ball and springs back when pressed lightly.

Turn dough in 2–3 teaspoons of oil in the cleaned, dry bowl, cover with cling film and leave in a warm draught-free place for about 30 minutes. Knead the risen dough lightly, then shape.

To shape and bake pizzas: Roll dough into thin circles, according to the number and size of pizzas you require. Place on sprayed pizza pans, Teflon liners, baking paper, or well oiled oven slides.

Add your favourite toppings (page 22) and bake at 225°C until the underside is brown. For crisp, very thin pizza bake before (and after) adding topping.

Pita Bread

To shape and bake pita breads: Cut the dough into 8 even pieces, then roll each piece out on a well-floured board, adding extra flour as needed, into a 15cm–18cm circle, then leave to stand for at least 10 minutes.

Heat the oven to its highest temperature, with an oven tray on a rack in the middle of the oven, and, if you have it, a cast iron pan or griddle on the rack below the middle. (This heats up and compensates for heat loss when the oven door is opened.)

Slide the first shaped pita bread onto a piece of floured cardboard, then, opening the oven door as briefly as possible, slide the bread onto the hot oven tray. In 1–2 minutes the bread should puff up dramatically, then collapse a little.

Lift out with tongs after 2–3 minutes and put the next pita bread in to cook. Pile the hot breads in a plastic bag so they do not dry out.

Bread Sticks & Broccoli Cheese Bread

Pizza dough is easy to make and work with. Use it when you feel like experimenting! We found that it was excellent for breadsticks, and also made unusual savoury rolls filled with vegetables and cheese.

Breadsticks

Bake breadsticks until they are completely dry, then pack them in airtight containers and store them until you want something to serve with soup.

Make the pizza dough recipe on page 20 in a bread machine or by hand.

Roll the dough into a rectangle 25cm x 30cm. Preferably using a cleaver or a heavy long-bladed knife, cut it into 25 strips, 1 cm wide and 30 cm long.

Arrange on baking paper or a Teflon liner, on one or more oven trays, about 1 cm apart. After you have cut and placed the last strip, brush with egg glaze (page 59) sprinkle with Parmesan, poppy or sesame seeds and bake at 150°C for 30–40 minutes, until they are evenly golden brown and crisp right through. (Start checking after 20 minutes, since ovens vary a great deal.)

Broccoli Cheese Bread

Although the idea of a vegetable-filled bread may seem rather odd, this is one of our favourite breads — its bright green filling is both attractive and unusual.

Make the pizza dough on page 20 in a bread machine or by hand.

Make the filling while the dough rises.

Filling:

1 onion, chopped
¼ cup olive oil
500g broccoli
¼ tsp oreganum
2 –3 Tbsp water
½ tsp salt
freshly ground black pepper
2 cups grated tasty cheese

In a medium pot cook the onion in the oil until transparent but not browned. Cut or break the broccoli heads into small (almond-size) florets. Peel and chop all the stems into pieces the same size. Add to the onion with the oreganum and water. Cover and cook over high heat for 2–3 minutes, until the broccoli is barely tender and the water has evaporated. Add the seasonings and cool.

After the dough has risen for the last time, roll it out on a floured board until it is about 40cm x 40cm. Arrange cooled broccoli over the dough, leaving 2cm clear along one side. Dampen this strip with cold water. Cover the broccoli with the grated cheese and roll up (like a sponge roll) clear side last.

Cut the roll into 16 even pieces. Place cut side up, in a buttered or oiled 23cm square cake pan. Cover and leave to rise in a warm draught-free place for about 30 minutes, or until double original size.

Sprinkle with extra grated tasty or Parmesan cheese and bake at 200°C for 30 minutes or nicely browned. Serve warm.

Calzone & Stromboli

Try these fashionable foods, using pizza dough in quite different ways. These recipes are sure to be popular with all age groups. Enclose whatever fillings you like in the pizza dough.

Calzone

Calzone is a pizza folded in half and sealed, before it is baked.

Make the pizza dough recipe on page 20, in a bread machine or by hand. After the dough has risen for the last time, cut into 8 even pieces. Roll each piece into a circle 20cm across, adding enough flour to stop it sticking to the rolling pin and work surface.

Cover half of each circle with your choice of pizza toppings or the filling for the Broccoli Cheese Bread (page 21) leaving a small uncovered rim. Moisten the rim with water then fold the uncovered half over the covered half and seal the edges. Lift onto an oven slide, cut several air vents, then leave to rise for about 10 minutes.

Bake at 220°C for about 10 minutes, and serve warm.

Stromboli

This is wonderfully tasty and portable! Made from thin layers of pizza dough and your favourite fillings, Stromboli is rolled up just like a strudel.

Make the pizza dough on page 20 in a bread machine or by hand. After the dough has risen for the last time, cut the dough in two. Working on a well floured bench roll the dough very thinly into a rectangle 40cm x 50cm making sure the dough does not stick.

Filling A: ¼ cup each of diced ham, diced salami, grated tasty cheese and Parmesan cheese

Filling B: 2–3 Tbsp basil pesto, ¼ cup each of sundried tomato paste, diced salami, diced ham and 1 cup grated tasty cheese

Spread the ingredients for either filling over the dough, then roll up as you would a sponge roll.

Lift the filled roll carefully onto an oven tray lined with baking paper or a Teflon liner, so the join is underneath.

Bake at 200°C for about 12 minutes or until golden brown. Serve warm or cold, cut in diagonal slices.

PIZZA TOPPING SUGGESTIONS

- Tomato paste, sundried tomato paste, dried tomato pesto, sliced tomatoes, drained canned seasoned tomatoes
- Red, yellow and green peppers, roasted red and orange pepper strips and eggplant
- Onion slices, caramelised onions, chopped spring onions, roasted garlic
- Sliced mushrooms, sliced/whole olives, fresh and dried herbs, artichoke hearts
- Anchovy fillets, salmon and shrimps, salami, ham, bacon, turkey and chicken
- Mozzarella, grated tasty cheese, Camembert and Brie, Parmesan, Feta

Stromboli, Pizza, Broccoli and Cheese Bread

Sourdough Breads

Sourdough Starter

We may buy the yeast we need without a second thought, but not so long ago, the only yeast available to people in isolated places was a homemade "starter", a flour and water mixture in which wild yeasts were grown.

The yeasts in this starter mixture were left to grow and multiply, in a jar or crock which was kept in a cool place in summer and a warm place in winter.

As some of this starter was used to rise bread, more flour and water was added to feed the remaining yeasts. Good starters (which made well-risen breads with a good flavour and a texture) were treasured by their owners, used for many years, and passed on to friends and relations.

On standing, a starter turns sour, and gives bread made from it an interesting tangy flavour, much sought after today in places such as San Francisco.

The sourdough starter we make is more refined than that described! Rather than starting with wild yeasts which float around in our kitchens, we start with a little bread yeast and grow it in a flour mixture in a very clean, carefully covered container.

The resulting starter works well, producing bread with an interesting sour flavour. If we use this up or let it die and make another starter, this will probably taste slightly different - it may be even better or it may not!

To prepare a simple starter, mix the following in a clean jar, leaving about $\frac{1}{4}$ of the jar for headspace.

2 cups Champion High Grade Flour
1 cup low fat milk or unsweetened yoghurt
1 cup water
1 tsp active dried yeast

Cover the jar and leave it in a warm room, out of the sun, for 4–7 days, depending on the temperature. Each day, stir the starter with a clean spoon.

For the first few days it may have a tendency to bubble up and overflow, but it will quieten down and become thinner after a few days. Refrigerate it in a lidded jar after it smells definitely sour and has a clear layer on top.

Keep it free from contamination. A slight greyish colour is fine, but if it develops a nasty smell or changes colour, especially to pink or purple, throw it out and start again.

To use the starter, stir well and pour off what you need. Replace each cup used with a cup of water mixed with a cup of high grade flour. Leave the jar at room temperature for a day before using more starter or refrigerating it again.

If you do not use your starter regularly, throw out or give away a cupful of it once a week and add fresh flour and water as above.

Bread made with only a starter needs a long rising time. Extra yeast is often used to speed up the process, and the starter is used for the characteristic flavour it provides.

Sourdough Bread

If you like the 'tang' and texture of sourdough breads, this recipe is for you! You can control the degree of sourness by increasing or decreasing the length of time that the sourdough mixture sits at room temperature before baking.

Makes a large loaf or 16 rolls:

1½ cups sourdough starter (page 25)
½ cup milk
1 Tbsp oil
1 Tbsp sugar
1 tsp salt
3½ cups Champion High Grade Flour
2 tsp Surebake yeast

Bread Machine Instructions

For a very sour flavour, mix the first five ingredients in the bread machine, put the flour and yeast on top, then leave everything to stand at room temperature for up to 8 hours, setting the timer mode.

Otherwise, just add all ingredients in the order suggested by the manufacturer and start the machine. Use the NORMAL/WHITE bread cycle, and MEDIUM crust settings (or use the DOUGH cycle and shape and bake by hand).

Handmade Bread Instructions

Combine the first five ingredients in a large bowl with half the flour. Add the Surebake yeast and mix thoroughly. Cover and leave for 15 minutes or longer in a warm place.

Add the rest of the flour and stir to make a soft dough, adding a little extra warm water or flour if necessary, to make a dough just firm enough to knead.

Knead with the dough hook of an electric mixer or by hand on a lightly floured surface for 10 minutes, until the dough forms a soft ball which is smooth and satiny, and springs back when pressed gently.

Turn the dough in 2–3 tsp oil in the cleaned dry bowl, cover with cling film and leave in a warm draught-free place for 30 minutes. Lightly knead the dough, and then shape as desired.

Shaping and baking

Roll the dough into one large round ball (standing in a 20–25 cm cake tin) or divide it evenly into 16 and roll into small round rolls.

Leave to rise in a warm draught-free place for 40 minutes, slash tops with a very sharp blade if desired, then leave 20 minutes longer or until double original size.

Bake at 210°C, 10–12 minutes for rolls or about 30 minutes for a large loaf, until bread is evenly brown, top and bottom. For a hard crust, mist with a water spray before and during the first few minutes of cooking or put a roasting pan containing boiling water 1cm deep in the bottom of the oven 1 minute before you put the bread in.

Note: Don't forget to replenish or "feed" your starter by adding 1½ cups of flour and 1½ cups of water.

Sourdough Focaccia

In days gone by, doughs were risen by adding a little uncooked bread dough reserved from the previous day's baking, or by adding "sourdough" starter. As well as helping to rise this popular bread, the sourdough gives it a lovely flavour.

Makes 2 flat loaves about 20cm x 30cm:

1 tsp active dried yeast
1 cup sourdough starter (page 25)
1 cup warm water
1 Tbsp sugar
1 tsp salt
3 cups Champion High Grade Flour

1–2 Tbsp olive oil   *Sliced black olives*
coarse salt   *Pesto*
Fresh rosemary   *Parmesan cheese, etc*

Bread Machine Instructions

Carefully measure the first six ingredients into a 750g capacity bread machine, in the order specified by the manufacturer.

Set to the DOUGH cycle and START. When the dough cycle is complete, shape and bake as below.

Handmade Bread Instructions

Measure sourdough starter, warm water, sugar and salt together into a large bowl, sprinkle over the yeast and leave to stand for 5 minutes. Add half the high grade flour, mix thoroughly, cover then leave to stand for 15 minutes or longer in a warm place.

Stir in the remaining flour, adding a little extra warm water or high grade flour if necessary, to make a dough just firm enough to knead.

Knead with the dough hook on an electric mixer or by hand on a lightly floured surface for 10 minutes, adding extra flour if necessary, until the dough forms a soft ball which springs back when pressed gently.

Turn dough in 2–3 teaspoons of oil in a clean, dry bowl. Cover with cling film and leave to stand for at least an hour. (The longer the dough stands, the better the flavour. It will keep in the refrigerator for 12–18 hours.) After standing knead lightly for about a minute.

Shaping and Baking

Divide the dough in half and roll each piece into a rectangle about 20 x 30 cm. Press each gently into an olive-oiled rectangular baking pan about the same size, making "finger hole" depressions all over the surface.

Spread with one or more of the listed toppings, letting some of the mixture fill the finger holes. Sprinkle with Parmesan cheese or coarse (rock) salt.

Leave to rise in a warm, draught-free place for 30–60 minutes, then drizzle with a little more olive oil and bake at 220°C for 10–15 minutes or until golden brown top and bottom. Serve warm, cut in fingers or rectangles, soon after cooking.

Note: Don't forget to replenish your starter by adding another cup of flour and a cup of water.

Focaccia

We're not sure exactly what it is about these Italian-style flat breads that makes them so appealing, but this is another of our favourites. Try it plain, or with some of our favourite toppings, but really these are only a start...

Makes one loaf about 22cm x 32cm:

2 tsp Surebake yeast
1½ cups water
1 Tbsp sugar
1 tsp salt
1 Tbsp olive oil
3 cups Champion High Grade Flour
1 tsp oreganum
1 Tbsp olive oil
coarse (rock) salt

Bread Machine Instructions

Carefully measure the first seven ingredients into a 750g capacity bread machine, in the order specified by the manufacturer.

Set to the DOUGH cycle and START. When the cycle is complete shape and bake as described below.

Handmade Bread Instructions

Measure the first five ingredients into a large bowl with 1½ cups high grade flour and mix thoroughly. Cover and leave for 15 minutes or longer in a warm place.

Stir in the remaining 1½ cups flour and oreganum, adding a little extra warm water or bread flour if necessary to make a dough just firm enough to knead.

Knead with the dough hook of an electric mixer or by hand on a lightly floured surface for 10 minutes, adding extra flour if necessary, until the dough forms a soft dough which springs back when pressed gently.

Turn the dough in 2–3 teaspoons of oil in the cleaned, dry bowl, cover with cling film and leave in a warm draught-free place for about 30 minutes.

Knead the oiled dough lightly in the bowl for about a minute.

Shaping and Baking

Turn the dough out onto a lightly floured board and roll into a rectangle about 20cm x 30cm. Place on a well oiled oven slide or in a sponge roll tin and leave to rise in a warm, draught-free place for about an hour or until double the original size.

Pour the second quantity of oil evenly over the surface and poke the loaf with two fingers at intervals over the surface. Sprinkle with rock salt or any of the following toppings.

2 tablespoons each pesto and olive oil mixed
    to a paste with ¼ cup Parmesan cheese
coarsely chopped sundried tomatoes
anchovies
sliced or whole black olives

Bake at 225°C for 15 minutes or until golden brown top and bottom.

Garlic & Olive Bread

Even if you do not like olives we think you will enjoy the savoury, but not overpowering flavour of this soft, crusty bread. Serve with Mediterranean food, enjoy it by itself, or use it to make the most delicious crostini we have ever tasted.

Makes one large round or brick-shaped loaf (6–8 cup pan):

3 tsp Surebake yeast

1¼ cups warm water

2 Tbsp olive oil

2 tsp sugar

1 tsp salt

¼ cup non-fat dried milk powder

3 cups Champion High Grade Flour

¼ cup grated Parmesan cheese

2 cloves garlic, chopped

1 Tbsp chopped fresh basil

1 tsp fresh thyme leaves

¼ cup chopped black olives

Bread Machine Instructions

Carefully measure all the ingredients into a 750g capacity bread machine, in the order specified by the manufacturer.

Set to the NORMAL/WHITE bread cycle, MEDIUM crust and START. This is a good timer bread.

Handmade Bread Instructions

Measure the first six ingredients into a large bowl. Add 1½ cups of the high grade flour and mix thoroughly. Cover and leave for 15 minutes or longer in a warm place.

Stir in the rest of the flour and the remaining ingredients, adding a little warm water or flour, if necessary, to make a dough just firm enough to knead.

Knead with the dough hook of an electric mixer or by hand on a lightly floured surface for 10 minutes, adding extra flour if necessary, until dough forms a soft ball which springs back when pressed gently.

Turn the dough in 1–2 teaspoons of oil in the cleaned, dry bowl, then cover with cling film and leave in a warm draught-free place for about 30 minutes.

Lightly knead the oiled dough in the bowl for about a minute, then turn out onto a lightly floured surface.

Shaping and Baking

For a round loaf, shape into a ball and flatten slightly onto a lightly oiled oven tray. For a loaf shape, pat or roll into a square a little longer than the pan, then roll up into a cylinder. Place the shaped dough into the buttered or sprayed pan.

Leave to rise in a warm draught-free place for about an hour, or until double its original size.

Brush with milk or egg glaze (page 59) if desired, then bake at 200°C for about 35 minutes until the sides and bottom of the loaf is brown and the loaf sounds hollow when tapped.

Crostini: To make Crostini from the Olive and Garlic Bread cut into 5mm slices, brush lightly with olive oil and bake at 150°C on oven trays for about 7 minutes or until golden brown and crisp. Cool before storing in an airtight container.

Ciabatta

This is one of several authentic Italian recipes translated for us by some very generous volunteers. Using a traditional approach this crusty bread is made in two stages, started one day, fermented over-night then completed and baked the next.

Makes a large flat loaf:

1 tsp active dried yeast

1½ cups warm water

2½ cups Champion High Grade Flour

2 Tbsp gluten flour

2 tsp active dried yeast

½ cup warm water

2 tsp malt

1½ tsp salt

1 cup Champion High Grade Flour

Bread Machine Instructions

Carefully measure the first four ingredients into a 750g capacity bread machine, in the order specified by the manufacturer. Set to the DOUGH cycle and START. When the cycle is complete place the dough in a large bowl, cover and leave to rise at room temperature for at least 12 hours.

After rising put the dough back into the bread machine with the remaining five ingredients. Set to the DOUGH cycle and START. Check after two minutes mixing — the dough should be very wet, barely forming a ball while the paddle is turning. When it stops the dough should flow to the edges of the bowl. If too firm, add water a little at a time until it is wet enough. When the cycle is complete, shape and bake as below.

Handmade Bread Instructions

In a large bowl sprinkle the first measure of yeast over the warm water and leave to stand for several minutes before adding the first quantity of flour and the gluten. Mix thoroughly, cover with cling film and leave to rise at room temperature for at least 12 hours.

In the large bowl of an electric mixer fitted with a dough hook, combine the remaining ingredients with the risen dough mixture and knead well. The dough should be too soft to knead by hand, flowing to the edges of the bowl when you turn off the mixer. Add extra warm water if necessary. Knead for 10 minutes. Remove the dough hook, cover the bowl with cling film and leave in a warm draught-free place for 30–40 minutes.

Shaping and Baking

Gently tip the very soft dough onto a well-floured oven tray covered with with baking paper or a Teflon liner, taking care not to knock the air from the dough. Sprinkle generously with flour and shape into an oblong 35cm–40cm long and 20cm wide. Leave to rise in a warm draught-free place for 40–50 minutes. Heat the oven to 240°C. To ensure a good crust put a roasting pan containing 1cm of hot water in the bottom of the oven five minutes before you put in the bread. Bake for 20–25 minutes, (removing the roasting pan of water after 10 minutes) until the loaf is crusty and evenly browned top and bottom, and sounds hollow when tapped. Leave the cooked bread to cool in the switched-off oven with the door open for 5–10 minutes.

French Bread

It is hard to believe that such a basic dough can produce such delicious crusty French bread. Leaving the dough to stand overnight requires a little patience and some forethought, but in the end it's worth the wait.

Makes one large or two smaller baguettes:

2 tsp active dried yeast

1¼ cups warm water

2 tsp sugar

1½ tsp salt

3 cups Champion High Grade Flour

Bread Machine Instructions

Carefully measure all the ingredients into a 750g capacity bread machine, in the order specified by the manufacturer.

Set to the DOUGH cycle and START. When the cycle is complete, allow to stand as described below before kneading, etc.

Handmade Bread Instructions

Measure the first four ingredients into a large bowl with 1½ cups of the high grade flour and mix thoroughly. Cover and leave for 15 minutes in a warm place.

Stir in the remaining flour and a little extra flour or water if necessary to make a dough just firm enough to knead.

Knead with the dough hook of an electric mixer or by hand on a lightly floured board for 10 minutes, until the dough forms a soft ball which springs back when lightly pressed.

Rising, Shaping and Baking

Turn dough in 2–3 teaspoons of oil in a large, clean, dry bowl. Cover with cling film and leave for at least 2 hours or preferably overnight **at room temperature**. It may be necessary to "punch" (or press) the dough down several times during this period.

Knead the dough very lightly in the bowl then turn out onto a lightly floured board. Roll and shape the dough into one long characteristic French "cigar" shaped loaf (or divide the dough in half to make two smaller loaves).

Leave to rise **at room temperature** for about 1–1½ hours or until about doubled in size. With a very sharp knife make a series of 4-5 diagonal slashes about 5mm deep on the top of the loaf or loaves.

Heat the oven to 220°C and at least five minutes before the bread is due to go into the oven put a roasting pan containing 1cm of boiling water in the bottom of the oven. (To get a really chewy crust, spray the loaf with a fine spray of water before putting in the oven then spray again after 2 minutes.)

Bake for 15 minutes, removing the roasting pan of water from the oven after 10 minutes. The loaf or loaves should be golden brown and sound hollow when tapped. Eat within 12 hours of baking.

Note: For a loaf with a more open texture, try adding 2 tablespoons of gluten with the flour. Add extra water as necessary, probably about ¼ cup.

Cottage Cheese Bread

This "nearly white" loaf keeps well, staying fresh for two or three days. Nobody will guess what it is that makes the loaf so moist and delicious!

Makes a "cottage" loaf 20cm across:

3 tsp Surebake yeast
½ cup cottage cheese
1 large egg
¾ cup warm water
2 Tbsp lecithin granules or oil
1 Tbsp sugar
1½ tsp salt
2½ cups Champion High Grade Flour
½ cup Champion Wholemeal Flour
2 Tbsp non-fat milk powder, optional

Bread Machine Instructions

Carefully measure all the ingredients into a 750g capacity bread machine, in the order specified by the manufacturer.

Set to the NORMAL/WHITE bread cycle, MEDIUM crust and START (or use the DOUGH cycle and shape and bake by hand as described below).

Handmade Bread Instructions

Measure the first seven ingredients into a large bowl. Add 1½ cups of the measured high grade flour and the milk powder (if using) and mix thoroughly. Cover and leave for 15 minutes or longer in a warm place.

Stir in the remaining flour, adding a little extra warm water or high grade flour if necessary, to make a dough just firm enough to knead.

Knead with the dough hook of an electric mixer, or by hand on a lightly floured surface for 10 minutes, adding extra flour if necessary, until the dough forms a soft ball which springs back when pressed.

Turn dough in a little oil in the cleaned, dry bowl, cover, and leave in a warm draught-free place for about 30 minutes.

Knead the oiled dough lightly in the bowl for a minute then turn out onto a lightly floured surface.

Shaping and Baking

Shape ¾ of the dough into a ball then flatten with the palm of your hand until it is about 15 cm in diameter. Roll the remaining ¼ of dough into a ball about 9 cm across. Lightly dampen the surface of the large ball with a little water, lie the smaller ball of dough on top then press your finger through the small ball to the centre of the large one, leaving a hole through the centre.

Leave to rise in a warm draught-free place for about an hour, or until double the original size.

For a crisp crust, spray with a fine spray of water or for a thin glazed crust brush with milk or an egg glaze (page 59) and bake at 200°C for 15–30 minutes, until evenly golden brown and hollow sounding when tapped. Longer cooking will make a thicker crust.

High Protein Bread

This nicely flavoured bread, derived from a recipe developed by Cornell University, has several added high-protein ingredients, and produces a large, extra-nutritious well-risen loaf, white enough to please fussy children.

Makes a large loaf (6 - 8 cup pan):

3 tsp Surebake yeast

1½ cups warm water

2 Tbsp lecithin granules or oil

2 Tbsp honey

1½ tsp salt

½ cup non-fat milk powder

2 cups Champion High Grade Flour

1 Tbsp gluten flour, optional

1½ cups Champion Wholemeal Flour

½ cup each soya flour and wheatgerm

Bread Machine Instructions

Carefully measure all the ingredients into a 750g capacity bread machine, in the order specified by the manufacturer. (If you add the gluten flour, add an extra two tablespoons of water.)

Set to the NORMAL/WHITE bread cycle, MEDIUM crust and START (or use the DOUGH cycle and shape and bake by hand). This is a good timer bread.

Handmade Bread Instructions

Measure the first seven ingredients plus the gluten flour if you are adding it into a large bowl and mix thoroughly. Cover and leave for 15 minutes in a warm place.

Add the remaining ingredients with a little extra flour or warm water if necessary, to make a dough just firm enough to knead.

Knead with the dough hook of an electric mixer or by hand on a lightly floured surface for 10 minutes, adding extra flour if necessary, until the dough forms a soft ball which springs back when lightly pressed.

Turn in 2–3 teaspoons of oil in the cleaned, dry bowl, cover with cling film and leave in a warm draught-free place for about 30 minutes.

Knead the oiled dough lightly in the bowl for a minute, then turn out onto a lightly floured surface and roll or pat out into a square a little longer than the baking tin. Roll into a cylinder, then put into the buttered or sprayed bread pan, pressing it into the corners and smoothing the top. (Or shape into a braid, a large round loaf or rolls, page 58.)

Leave to stand in a warm draught-free place for about 60 minutes or until double in size.

Bake at 200°C for 30–40 minutes or until the unmoulded loaf has browned sides, the bottom crust is browned and the unmoulded loaf sounds hollow when tapped.

Five Seed Bread

Five different types of seed are added to this bread which has, as a result, an unusual texture and appearance as well as an interesting flavour. It keeps well for several days and makes good toast, too.

Makes a large loaf (8 cup pan) or 4 small loaves (2 cup pans):

3 tsp Surebake yeast
1¼ cups plus 2 Tbsp warm water
2 tsp sugar
1½ tsp salt
2 Tbsp lecithin granules or oil
1½ cups Champion High Grade Flour
1½ cups Champion Wholemeal Flour
¼ cup each sunflower, pumpkin, poppy
    and raw or toasted sesame seeds*
2 Tbsp linseed(s)

Bread Machine Instructions

Carefully measure all the ingredients into a 750g capacity bread machine, in the order specified by the manufacturer.

Set to the NORMAL/WHITE cycle, MEDIUM crust and START (or use the DOUGH cycle and shape as described below). This is a good timer bread.

Handmade Bread Instructions

Measure the first six ingredients into a large bowl. Mix thoroughly and then cover and leave for 15 minutes or longer in a warm place.

Stir in the wholemeal flour and the seeds to make a soft dough. If necessary, add extra bread flour until you have a dough just firm enough to knead.

Knead with the dough hook of an electric mixer, or by hand on a lightly floured surface for 10 minutes, adding extra flour if needed, until the dough forms a soft ball and springs back when pressed gently.

Turn the dough in 2–3 teaspoons of oil in the cleaned, dry bowl, cover with cling film and leave in a warm draught-free place for 30 minutes.

Knead the oiled dough lightly in the bowl for a minute.

Shaping and baking

Pat the dough into a square a little longer than the baking pan. Roll the dough into a cylinder, then press into the buttered or sprayed bread pan, pressing it into the corners and levelling the top. Or, if using the small pans, divide the dough into four, then shape each piece as above.

Leave to rise in a warm draught-free place for about an hour or until double the original size.

If desired, brush with milk or egg glaze (page 59) then sprinkle with any of the seeds used in the loaf.

Bake at 200°C for 15–35 minutes, or until each unmoulded loaf has a browned bottom and sides, and sounds hollow when tapped.

* For maximum flavour, toast sesame seeds in a dry frypan or under the grill before using them.

Beer Braid

Try making this bread with different beers. Lager will produce a light coloured loaf with a subtle flavour, while darker beers will produce darker bread with stronger flavour.

Makes a large loaf or a braid 35 cm long:

3 tsp Surebake yeast
350 ml* beer or lager
1 Tbsp sugar
1 tsp salt
2 Tbsp lecithin granules or oil
1 cup Champion Wholemeal Flour
2 cups Champion High Grade Flour

350 ml is 1½ cups less 5 tsp! (flat beer works in this recipe, too)

Bread Machine Instructions

Carefully measure all the ingredients into a 750g capacity bread machine, in the order specified by the manufacturer.

Set to the NORMAL/WHITE cycle, MEDIUM crust and START (or use DOUGH cycle and shape by hand as described below). This is a good timer bread.

Handmade Bread Instructions

Measure the first six ingredients into a large bowl and mix thoroughly. Cover and leave 15 minutes or longer in a warm place.

Add the high grade flour and stir to make a soft dough. If necessary, add enough extra high grade flour until you have a dough just firm enough to knead.

Knead with the dough hook of an electric mixer, or by hand on a lightly floured surface, for 10 minutes, until the dough forms a soft ball which springs back when pressed gently.

Turn the dough in 2–3 teaspoons of oil in the cleaned, dry bowl, cover with cling film and leave in a warm draught-free place for 30 minutes. Knead the oiled dough lightly in the bowl for a minute.

Shaping and baking

Shape the dough to fit into a loaf pan (see details on page 33) or divide the dough into three. Roll each piece of dough into a 40cm long "sausage", and place the three lightly floured sausages, side by side on baking paper, a Teflon liner, or a lightly floured oven tray. For the neatest, most regular braid, start from the middle and plait from the middle to one end, then turn the dough around and plait from the middle to the other end. This is a little tricky, as you have to work the strands in the opposite order to keep the pattern intact. If you prefer to, just plait from one end to the other.

Leave to rise in a warm draught-free place for about an hour, or until the dough has approximately doubled in size.

Spray with water for a crustier braid, or brush with milk or egg glaze (page 59). Bake at 200°C for 20–45 minutes (use the longer time for a heavier crust) until the loaf is browned, top and bottom.

Double Corn Bread

Cornmeal gives this bread a lovely colour, and the creamed corn makes it wonderfully moist and delicious.
Try it with and without the herbs, alone or with your favorite Tex-Mex food.

Makes a large loaf (8 cup pan):

3 tsp Surebake yeast
½ cup canned creamed corn
1¼ cups warm water
2 tsp sugar
1½ tsp salt
2 Tbsp lecithin granules or oil
2 cups Champion High Grade Flour
1 cup Champion Wholemeal Flour
½ cup fine or coarse cornmeal
½ cup grated cheese
1 tsp each cumin & oreganum
pinch of chili powder
2 Tbsp coarse cornmeal, optional

Bread Machine Instructions

Carefully measure all the ingredients into a 750g capacity bread machine, in the order specified by the manufacturer.

Set to the NORMAL/WHITE bread cycle, MEDIUM crust and START (or use the DOUGH cycle and shape and bake by hand). This is a good timer bread.

Handmade Bread Instructions

Measure the first six ingredients into a large bowl. Add 1 cup of the high grade flour, and mix thoroughly. Cover and leave for 15 minutes or longer in a warm place.

Add the remaining high grade flour and all the other ingredients and stir to make a soft dough, adding extra flour if necessary.

Knead with the dough hook of an electric mixer or by hand on a lightly floured surface for 10 minutes, adding extra flour if necessary, until the dough forms a soft ball which springs back when pressed gently.

Turn in 2–3 teaspoons of oil in the cleaned, dry bowl, cover with cling film and leave in a warm draught-free place for 30–40 minutes.

Knead the dough in the bowl for a minute then turn out onto a lightly floured surface.

Pat or roll the dough into a square a little longer than the baking pan then roll into a cylinder. Place the dough in the buttered or sprayed bread pan, pressing it into the corners and levelling the top.

Leave to rise in a warm draught-free place for about an hour, or until the dough has approximately doubled in size.

Dampen the top and sprinkle with a little coarse cornmeal if you like, then bake at 200°C for about 30 minutes, until the crust is golden and the unmoulded loaf has a browned bottom and sides and sounds hollow when tapped on the bottom.

Variations: Shape the dough to make a round loaf or form it into two long "sausages" each 50cm long, then twist these together loosely to make a twisted loaf. Place on a sprayed or oiled baking tray to rise, finish and bake as described above for the loaf in the pan.

Rice Bread

This is a good way to use up left-over cooked rice. Strangely, you won't really notice the rice in the "almost white" bread but it gives the crust some real crunch! The rice also keeps the loaf moist so it stays fresh for several days.

Makes a large loaf (6 - 8 cup pan):

3 tsp Surebake yeast
1¼ cups warm water
2 tsp sugar
1½ tsp salt
2 Tbsp lecithin granules or oil
3 Tbsp non-fat milk powder
1 cup Champion Wholemeal Flour
2 cups Champion High Grade Flour
1 cup cooked rice

in the rice may vary, try adding 1 cup plus 2 Tbsp of water initially, adding the additional 2 Tbsp of water if the dough is too dry. Set to the NORMAL/WHITE bread cycle, MEDIUM crust and START (or use the DOUGH cycle and shape and bake by hand.) Once you have worked out the correct amount of water for your machine, this is a good timer bread.

Handmade Bread Instructions

Measure the first seven ingredients into a large bowl and mix thoroughly. Cover and leave to stand for 15 minutes or longer in a warm place.

[...] flour and cooked rice, [...] water or enough extra [...] dough just firm [...]

[...] gh hook of an electric [...] a lightly floured [...]tes, until the dough is smooth and satiny, and springs back when pressed gently.

Turn in 2–3 teaspoons of oil in the cleaned, dry bowl, cover with cling film and leave in a warm draught-free place for 30–40 minutes.

Knead the dough lightly in the bowl for a minute then turn out onto a lightly floured surface, pat into a square a little longer than the baking pan. Roll the dough into a cylinder then put it in the sprayed or buttered baking pan, pushing it into the corners and leveling the top.

Leave to rise in a warm draught-free place for about an hour, or until the dough has approximately doubled in size.

If desired, brush with milk or egg glaze (page 59) then bake at 200°C for about 30 minutes, or until the unmoulded loaf has browned on its bottom and sides and sounds hollow when tapped.

[handwritten note:] I added 1 cup plus 3 table water 28.10.08 - Crust wasn't crunchy Try 2 table of water

37

Potato Bread

Not only does the addition of potato to bread help make it seem more substantial, but it also helps to hold in moisture, keeping the bread fresh for longer.

Makes a large Cottage loaf 23 cm across:

3 tsp Surebake yeast
1¾ cups warm water
3 Tbsp lecithin granules or oil
1 Tbsp sugar
1½ tsp salt
1 cup Champion Wholemeal Flour
2 cups Champion High Grade Flour
1 cup instant potato flakes

Bread Machine Instructions

Carefully measure all the ingredients into a 750g capacity bread machine, in the order specified by the manufacturer.

Set to the NORMAL/WHITE bread cycle, MEDIUM crust and START (or use the DOUGH cycle and shape and rise the loaf by hand as described below). This is a good timer bread.

Handmade Bread Instructions

Measure the first six ingredients into a large bowl and mix thoroughly. Cover and leave for 15 minutes or longer in a warm place.

Stir in the high grade flour and the potato flakes and stir to make a soft dough, adding a little extra flour if necessary, making a dough just firm enough to turn out and knead.

Knead with the dough hook of an electric mixer or by hand on a lightly floured surface for 10 minutes, adding extra flour if necessary, until the dough forms a soft ball which springs back when pressed gently.

Turn the dough in 2–3 teaspoons of oil in the cleaned, dry bowl, cover with cling film and leave in a warm, draught-free place for 30 minutes.

Shaping and Baking

Knead the oiled dough lightly in the bowl for a minute, then gently form it into a large ball on a Teflon or baking paper lined (or well oiled) oven tray and leave to rise again in a warm draught-free place for about an hour or until the dough has doubled in size.

Lightly spray the top of the loaf with water and sprinkle evenly with flour, preferably using a flour shaker or a sieve. Cut shallow parallel lines about 2cm apart across the top of the loaf, then do the same again at right angles to them, making a checkerboard pattern.

Bake at 225°C for 20–30 minutes or until the loaf is evenly browned top and bottom, and sounds hollow when the centre of the bottom is tapped.

Note: Leave until cold before eating, since dried potato flakes sometimes give the freshly made warm bread an unusual flavour which disappears on cooling.

Kumara & Cumin Bread

Two of our favourites, kumara and cumin are certainly not considered everyday bread ingredients, but they produce loaves with a lovely moist texture, good keeping qualities, and a very pleasant aroma and flavour.

Makes a large loaf or 2 "Vienna" loaves:

3 tsp Surebake yeast

1¼ cups warm water

¾ cup cooked mashed kumara

1 large egg

2 Tbsp honey

1½ tsp salt

2 Tbsp lecithin granules or melted butter

2 Tbsp non-fat milk powder

1½ cups Champion High Grade Flour

1½ cups Champion Wholemeal Flour

2 tsp cumin seed, roasted

¼ tsp curry powder

Bread Machine Instructions

Carefully measure all the ingredients into a 750g capacity bread machine, in the order specified by the manufacturer. Set the machine to the NORMAL/WHITE bread setting, MEDIUM crust and START (or use the DOUGH setting and shape and bake as described below).

Check the dough after about 5 minutes of mixing. The dough should be a smooth ball — if it looks too wet and sticky add 1–2 tablespoons of flour and if too dry add similar amounts of water.

Handmade Bread Instructions

Measure the first nine ingredients into a large bowl. Mix thoroughly, cover, then leave for 15 minutes or longer in a warm place.

Stir in the wholemeal flour, cumin seed and curry powder. Mix to make a soft dough, adding extra flour if necessary, to make a dough just firm enough to knead. (Sometimes you may need to add a considerable amount of additional flour, depending on the moisture content of the kumara.)

Knead with the dough hook of an electric mixer or by hand on a lightly floured surface for 10 minutes, adding as much extra flour as necessary, to make a soft

dough which springs back when pressed gently. Turn dough in 2–3 teaspoons of oil in the cleaned, dry bowl, cover with cling film and leave in a warm draught-free place for 30 minutes.

Knead the oiled dough lightly in the bowl for a minute.

Shaping and baking

Divide the dough in half then pat each piece into an oval shape about 20 cm long and about 12 cm wide. Lift each loaf onto a lightly sprayed or oiled sponge roll tin then leave to rise for about 30 minutes or loaves are about one and a half times their original size.

Spray with a film of water, then dust with flour (shaken on from a sieve).

Bake at 200°C for 20–35 minutes, or until the crust is evenly golden brown, the crust firm, and the loaves sound hollow when tapped on the bottom.

Bagels

Let the plane to New York leave without you! Make your own wonderfully chewy bagels for about a tenth of the price of bought ones, in a surprisingly short time! Spoil yourself with the traditional toppings of cream cheese and smoked salmon. Bliss!

Makes 8 plump bagels:

3 tsp Surebake yeast
1¼ cups warm water
2 Tbsp honey
1½ tsp salt
1 cup Champion Wholemeal Flour
2 Tbsp gluten flour
2 cups Champion High Grade Flour

Bread Machine Instructions

Carefully measure all the ingredients into a 750g capacity bread machine, in the order specified by the manufacturer.

Set to the DOUGH cycle and START. Stop the machine and remove the dough 40 minutes after mixing starts, even though the cycle is not complete. Shape and bake by hand, following the instructions below.

Handmade Bread Instructions

Measure the first five ingredients into a large bowl and mix thoroughly. Cover and leave for 15 minutes or longer in a warm place.

Stir in the gluten and high grade flour, adding extra flour or water if necessary, until you have dough just firm enough to knead.

Knead with the dough hook of an electric mixer or by hand on a lightly floured surface for 10 minutes, until you have a soft dough which is smooth and satiny, and which springs back when pressed gently.

Turn the dough in 2–3 teaspoons of oil in the cleaned dry bowl, cover with cling film and leave in a warm draught-free place for 30 minutes.

Shaping and Baking

Knead dough lightly for a minute, then cut into 8 equal pieces. Roll each into a "snake" about 26cm long, then dampen the ends with water and press together firmly, forming rings. Place the rings on a sheet (or individual pieces) of oiled baking paper and leave for 10–15 minutes.

During this time bring a large pan containing water 5–10cm deep to the boil. Carefully lower 3 bagels at a time into the boiling water, lift away the paper, and cook for 30–45 seconds per side. Drain on paper towels, then put on a large baking tray lined with baking paper or a Teflon liner, leaving space for rising.

Brush as far down the sides as you can with egg glaze (page 59) and sprinkle with poppy or toasted sesame seeds.

Bake at 220°C for 10–12 minutes until browned top and bottom. Cool on a rack and serve warm or toasted within 24 hours of making, or freeze in an airtight container as soon as they are cold.

Bagels

Croissants

Croissants

Everybody's favourites! Although the recipe may seem complicated at first, once you have made these a few times you will become a dab hand! Follow the instructions carefully, rolling and folding the dough to produce light flaky layers.

Makes 10 –12 croissants:

3 tsp Surebake yeast
1 cup warm water
1 large egg
25g butter, melted
2 tsp sugar
1 tsp salt
¼ cup non fat milk powder
3–3 ½ cups Champion High Grade Flour
100–150g cold butter

Bread Machine Instructions

Add all the ingredients except the second measure of butter to a 750g capacity bread machine, in the order specified by the manufacturer.

Set to the DOUGH cycle and start. When the dough is completed, remove it from the machine, place in plastic bag and refrigerate for 10–15 minutes.

Handmade Dough Instructions

Measure the first seven ingredients into a large bowl. Add 1½ cups of the measured flour, mix thoroughly, cover, then leave to stand for 15 minutes or longer in a warm place.

Stir in the remaining flour to make a soft dough, adding more flour if necessary, until you have a dough just firm enough to knead.

Knead with the dough hook of an electric mixer, or by hand on a lightly floured surface for 10 minutes, adding extra flour if necessary, until the dough forms a soft ball which springs back when pressed gently.

Place in a plastic bag and refrigerate for 10–15 minutes.

Layering and Baking Instructions

While the dough cools, prepare the cold butter by placing it between two sheets of plastic or cling film. Using a rolling pin, roll the butter into a rectangle 10 x 15cm and 5–7mm thick then remove the film.

From this stage keep everything as cold as possible.

Turn the chilled dough onto a lightly floured board and roll into a rectangle 25 x 35cm. Lay the sheet of butter diagonally across this, (see diagram) then fold the corners of the dough over the rectangle of butter, so the butter is completely contained in an envelope of dough.

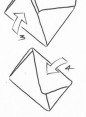

Place on a tray and refrigerate for 15 minutes.

Fold the chilled dough in half, so the short ends meet, and roll gently into a rectangle 30 x 20cm.

Next, fold the dough into thirds (see diagram) as you would fold a sheet of paper to put it into an envelope, and refrigerate for 10 minutes.

Roll the chilled dough out again into a 30 x 20cm rectangle, then fold into thirds as above. Roll out (to 30 x 20cm) and fold in thirds once more before refrigerating for another 10 minutes.

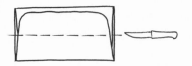

Cut the dough in half lengthwise, return half to the refrigerator, then roll the other into a rectangle 40cm x 20cm. With a sharp knife make diagonal cuts across the dough (see diagram) to make five or six fairly even triangles of dough.

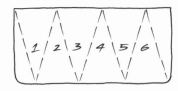

Starting with the short side of the dough triangle towards you roll up each triangle loosely, moistening the pointed end with a little cold water to seal it down.

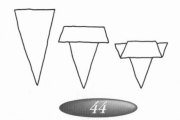

Bend the pointed ends inwards to form the traditional croissant shapes and lie these (with the pointed tips underneath) on a buttered or sprayed oven tray, allowing plenty of room for spreading.

Make another five or six croissants in the same way with the remaining dough, and put these on another baking tray.

Leave to rise in a warm draught-free place for 1–2 hours (or overnight in the refrigerator) until double their original volume.

Brush with egg glaze (page 59) and bake at 200°C for 15–20 minutes until golden brown top and underneath.

Cool on a rack. Serve warm with your favourite jam (and butter if you like) or split and add your favourite fillings for lunch.

Danish Pastries

Danish pastries are made from croissant dough which is really a buttery, yeast-based pastry.
It may be shaped in many ways to make these flaky, luxurious treats for weekend breakfasts and brunches. Here are two to try!

Almond Danish Pastries

Roll out the entire croissant dough to a 36 cm square. Trim the edges straight, then cut into nine 12cm squares.

To make an almond filling, beat together with a fork: 1 egg white or yolk (or half an egg), ½ cup ground almonds, ¼ cup sugar and a few drops of almond essence.

Put no more than a tablespoon of this filling in the middle of each square, then fold each corner over the filling and into the middle of the pastry, so the corners overlap slightly. Press the centre and outer edges firmly. Place each pastry in an individual pie pan if you have these, otherwise put on a lightly floured oven tray.

Bake at 200°C for 15–20 minutes or until evenly browned, putting a canned apricot half or other piece of fruit in the centre of the pastry after about 10 minutes if you like. Brush cooked pastries with sieved, heated apricot jam or apricot glaze while very hot.

Apple-filled "Snails"

Roll the croissant dough out into two rectangles each about 20 x 40 cm. Spread with the almond filling above, or with custard, leaving 2–3 cm clear on one long side of each rectangle of dough.

To make custard, mix together until smooth: 2 tablespoons each of sugar and cornflour, ¾ cup of milk and 1 egg. Heat gently until thick, stirring all the time, then add 1 teaspoon of butter.

Over the almond filling or cold custard, spread about a cup of well-drained stewed apple, ¼ cup of sugar and ½ cup of sultanas. Moisten the clear edges with water. Roll up, dampened edges last.

Cut each roll into 12–18 pinwheels or snails, place on baking-paper lined oven trays, in individual round pie pans, or arrange in baking-paper lined cake tins as for Cinnamon Swirls, page 56, then leave to rise at room temperature for 1–2 hours (or overnight in the refrigerator).

Bake at 200°C for about 15 minutes. Brush with sieved, heated apricot jam or apricot glaze while very hot.

Notes: We found that the Apricot Pastries unfolded if they were left to rise before baking. They kept their shapes best in individual pie pans.

The snails tended to unroll sometimes when baked on oven trays rather than in pans.

Experiment with other fillings and with different shapes if you like!

Always take care to keep the dough cool, and do not roll it too thinly, or you will lose the layered effect.

Brioche

How do we describe brioche? Perhaps a cross between bread and cake. Being neither sweet nor savoury Brioche are very versatile and can be enjoyed with coffee and jam for breakfast or served as rich dinner rolls.

Makes 8–10 brioche:

½ cup warm milk
3 large eggs
3 tsp Surebake yeast
75g butter, melted
¼ cup sugar
1 tsp salt
3 cups Champion Standard Plain Flour
    (plus ¼ cup if required)

Bread Machine Instructions

Carefully measure all the ingredients into a 750g capacity bread machine, in the order specified by the manufacturer.

Set to the DOUGH cycle, and start. Check the dough after about 3 minutes mixing. It should be soft, but if it looks too wet and sticky, add 2 tablespoons of the extra flour (repeat if necessary).

When the dough cycle is complete, remove the dough from the machine and transfer to a well oiled bowl. Refrigerate for at least one hour (or overnight), then shape and bake as below.

Handmade Bread Instructions

In a large bowl mix together the warm milk and eggs. Sprinkle on the yeast and leave to stand for 5 minutes. Add the sugar, salt and 1½ cups of flour, mix thoroughly, cover and leave for 15 minutes or longer in a warm place.

Add the butter and the remaining flour, then stir to make a soft dough, adding a little extra flour if necessary.

Knead with the dough hook of an electric mixer or by hand, on a lightly floured surface, for 10 minutes, until the dough forms a soft ball which is smooth and satiny, and springs back when lightly pressed.

Turn in 2–3 teaspoons of oil in the cleaned, dry bowl, cover with cling film and refrigerate for at least one hour (or overnight).

Shaping and Baking

Turn the dough out on a lightly floured surface and divide into 4–5 pieces, halve each of these to give a total of 8 or 10 equal pieces. Shape each piece into a ball, then with the side of your hand almost saw off ¼ of the dough. Pick the dough up by the "head" and place in a well oiled muffin tin or fluted brioche pan. Press the small ball (head) firmly onto the base so it looks like a small snowman.

Leave to rise in a warm draught-free place for about an hour, or until the dough has approximately doubled in size.

Brush with egg glaze (page 59) and bake at 180°C for about 15 minutes, or until golden brown on all surfaces.

Raisin & Nut Bread ✓

The addition of a few raisins and a handful of nuts make this bread something quite special. Try adding the cinnamon as well, if you want to fill the house with a wonderful aroma - it's great to wake up to!

Makes a large loaf (6 – 8 cup pan):

3 tsp Surebake yeast ✓

1 ¼ cups plus 2 Tbsp warm water ✓

2 Tbsp sugar

1 tsp salt

2 Tbsp lecithin granules or oil ✓

2 Tbsp non-fat milk powder

1½ cups Champion High Grade Flour

1½ cups Champion Wholemeal Flour

2 tsp cinnamon, optional

½ cup raisins + 3 table

¼ cup chopped nuts (eg walnuts or pecans)

put with everything

Bread Machine Instructions

Carefully measure all the ingredients into a 750g capacity bread machine, in the order specified by the manufacturer.

Set to the RAISIN BREAD (FRUIT LOAF) cycle, MEDIUM crust and START, adding

program 5.

the nuts and raisins when the machine beeps. This is a good timer bread. If using the timer, just place the raisins and nuts on top of everything else.

Handmade Bread Instructions

Measure the first seven ingredients into a large bowl and mix thoroughly. Cover and leave for 15 minutes or longer in a warm place.

Stir in the wholemeal flour, cinnamon (if using) and the raisins and nuts. Add extra flour if necessary to make a dough just firm enough to knead.

Knead with the dough hook of an electric mixer or by hand on a lightly floured surface for 10 minutes, adding extra flour if necessary, until the dough forms a soft ball which springs back when pressed gently.

Turn the dough in 2–3 teaspoons of oil in the cleaned, dry bowl, cover with cling film and leave in a warm draught-free place for 30 minutes.

Knead the oiled dough lightly in the bowl for a minute, then pat it into a square a little longer than the baking pan. Roll the dough into a cylinder, then put into the oiled or sprayed bread pan, pressing it into the corners and levelling the top.

Leave to rise in a warm draught-free place for about an hour, or until doubled in size.

If desired, brush with milk or with egg glaze (page 59) and bake at 200°C for about 30 minutes or until the unmoulded loaf has a browned bottom and sides and sounds hollow when tapped underneath.

Muesli Bread

Try muesli on a bread and butter plate for a change! This is a great breakfast bread, slightly sweet, with good flavour and texture.
For happy Monday morning faces, put the ingredients in your bread machine on Sunday night, and set the timer!

Makes a large loaf (6 – 8 cup pan):

3 tsp Surebake yeast
1½ cups warm water
2 Tbsp sugar
1 tsp salt
2 Tbsp lecithin granules or oil
1 cup Champion Wholemeal Flour
2 cups Champion High Grade Flour
1 cup toasted muesli

Bread Machine Instructions

Carefully measure all the ingredients into a 750g capacity bread machine, in the order specified by the manufacturer.

Set to the NORMAL/WHITE bread cycle, MEDIUM crust and START (or use the DOUGH cycle and shape by hand). This is a good timer bread.

Handmade Bread Instructions

Measure the first six ingredients into a large bowl. Mix thoroughly then cover and leave 15 minutes or longer in a warm place.

Stir in the high grade flour and muesli to make a soft dough. Add enough high grade flour to make a dough just firm enough to knead.

Knead with the dough hook of an electric mixer or by hand on a floured surface for 10 minutes, adding extra flour if necessary, until dough forms a soft ball and springs back when pressed gently.

Turn the dough in 2–3 teaspoons of oil in the cleaned, dry bowl, cover with cling film and leave in a warm draught-free place for about 30 minutes.

Knead the oiled dough in the bowl for a minute, pat it into a square a little longer than the baking pan, then roll into a cylinder and put it into the oiled or sprayed bread pan, pressing it into the corners and levelling the top. For something different, shape into rolls, a braid or round cottage loaf (see page 58).

Leave to rise in a warm, draught-free place for about an hour, or until double its original size.

If desired, brush with milk or egg glaze (page 59) sprinkle with sunflower or other seeds, and bake at 200°C – 210°C for about 30 minutes, until the unmoulded loaf has a browned bottom and sides, and sounds hollow when tapped.

Eat while warm with a little butter and honey. Use for toast the next day.

Fruity Oat Bread

This is a delicious fruity loaf with a golden brown "crumb" and a wonderful flavour. It stays nice and moist for a couple of days because of the oats. If you like the combination of almonds and fruit, try this special loaf!

Makes a medium-large loaf (6–8 cup pan):

3 tsp Surebake yeast

1¼ cups warm water

1 large egg

1 Tbsp honey

1 tsp salt

3 Tbsp lecithin granules or oil

3 Tbsp non-fat milk powder

1 cup Champion Wholemeal Flour

2 cups Champion High Grade Flour

1 cup rolled oats

½ cup each chopped dried apricots and
    Californian raisins

¼ cup slivered almonds, toasted

Bread Machine Instructions

Carefully measure all the ingredients into a 750g capacity bread machine, in the order specified by the manufacturer.

Set to the NORMAL/WHITE bread cycle, MEDIUM crust and START (or use the DOUGH cycle and shape and bake by hand as described below).

Handmade Bread Instructions

Measure the first eight ingredients into a large bowl and stir until smooth, then cover and leave for 15 minutes or longer in a warm place.

Add the high grade flour, rolled oats and the dried fruit and nuts. Stir together to make a soft dough, adding a little extra warm water or flour if necessary.

Knead with the dough hook of an electric mixer or by hand on a lightly floured surface for 10 minutes, adding extra flour if necessary, until the dough is smooth and satiny and forms a soft ball which springs back when pressed gently.

Clean and dry the bowl, add 1–2

teaspoons of oil and the dough, turning to coat it evenly. Cover with cling film and leave in a warm draught-free place for 30–40 minutes.

Lightly knead the oiled dough in the bowl for a minute, and then form it into a rectangle a little longer than the baking pan. Roll the dough into a cylinder and place this in the sprayed or oiled pan, pressing it into the corners and levelling the top.

Leave to rise in a warm draught-free place for about an hour, or until the dough has approximately doubled in size.

Bake at 180°C for 30–40 minutes, until the sides and bottom of the unmoulded loaf are golden brown and the loaf sounds hollow when tapped on the bottom.

Remove from the oven and brush with golden syrup glaze (page 59), if desired.

Hot Cross Buns

A wonderful treat for Easter (or anytime for that matter!), homemade Hot Cross Buns are well worth the effort. When time is short, make Easter buns (without crosses).

To make 16 – 20 Hot Cross Buns:

1/2 cup each warm milk and water
1/2 cup brown sugar
4 tsp active dried yeast
75g butter, barely melted
1 large egg
1 tsp salt
4 cups Champion High Grade Flour
1 Tbsp each mixed spice and cinnamon
1 tsp each ground cloves and vanilla
1 cup mixed fruit or currants

Bread Machine Instructions

Carefully measure all the ingredients into a 750g capacity bread machine, in the order specified by the manufacturer.

Set to the DOUGH cycle and start. (Add the mixed fruit at the beep if your machine does this.) When the cycle is complete, shape and bake as described below.

Handmade Bread Instructions

Measure the warm milk, water and one tablespoon of the brown sugar into a large bowl, warm or cool to body temperature, then sprinkle in the yeast granules. Stir after 2 minutes to ensure yeast has dissolved before adding 2 cups of the measured high grade flour. Cover and leave in a warm place for about 30 minutes.

In another bowl mix the melted butter and remaining brown sugar, then beat in the egg, salt, spices, vanilla and dried fruit. Add the risen yeast mixture and the remaining high grade flour and mix to make a dough just firm enough to knead, adding a little extra flour if necessary.

Knead with the dough hook of an electric mixer or by hand on a lightly floured surface for 10 minutes or until the dough forms a soft ball and springs back when lightly pressed.

Shaping and Baking

Divide the dough evenly into four pieces then each of these into 4 or 5. Shape each piece into a round ball (see details on page 18) and arrange in sprayed or Teflon-lined baking pans, or in a rectangular roasting pan, leaving about 1 cm between each bun. Cover with cling film and leave in a warm place until double in size.

If you want to add pastry crosses, rub 60g cold butter into 1 cup of high grade flour then add about 3 tablespoons of cold water to form a stiff dough. Roll very thinly then cut into strips, brush with beaten egg and place carefully on the risen buns, egg side down.

Bake at 225°C for 10–12 minutes or until lightly browned. Glaze immediately with a syrup made by bringing to the boil one tablespoon each of golden syrup, honey and water.

Hot Cross Buns

Festive Wreath

Festive Wreath

This wreath is something really special! It may seem rather complicated the first time you try it, but we think that it will be received so enthusiastically that you will want to make it again. Simplify the shaping if you like.

Dough:

3 tsp active dried yeast
1¼ cups warm milk
1 Tbsp sugar
1½ tsp salt
50g butter, softened
3 cups Champion Standard Plain Flour

Filling:

50g butter
2 Tbsp sugar
¼ cup Champion Standard Plain Flour
¾ tsp almond essence
½ cup each toasted almonds and dried apricots, chopped
¼ cup each red and green glace cherries, chopped

Bread Machine Instructions

Carefully measure all the ingredients into a 750g capacity bread machine, in the order specified by the manufacturer.

Set to the DOUGH cycle and START. When the cycle is complete, remove the dough and fill, shape and bake as described below.

Handmade Bread Instructions

Measure the first five ingredients into a large bowl with 1½ cups of the flour. Mix thoroughly then cover and leave for 15 minutes or longer in a warm place.

Add the remaining flour and stir to make a soft dough, adding a little extra flour if necessary, to make a dough just firm enough to knead. Knead with the dough hook of an electric mixer, or by hand on a lightly floured surface for 10 minutes, adding extra flour if necessary, until the dough forms a soft ball which springs back when pressed gently.

Turn the dough in 2 teaspoons of oil in the cleaned, dry bowl, cover with cling film and leave in a warm draught-free place for 30-40 minutes.

Filling, Shaping and Baking

Prepare the filling by beating together the softened butter, sugar, flour and essence, then fold in the fruit and nuts.

Knead the dough lightly for a minute then roll out into a rectangle 25 x 75 cm, on a well-floured surface.

Dot the filling evenly over the dough then roll up tightly, starting from a long edge. Cut the roll in half lengthwise using a sharp knife, then twist the two strands loosely together, cut sides out. Form into a ring, pinching the ends together, on a floured oven tray. Leave to rise in a warm, draught-free place for 40–60 minutes or until double its original size.

Brush lightly with egg glaze (page 59) and bake at 200°C for 20 minutes or until lightly browned. If you like, while warm, drizzle with icing made by mixing 1 cup sifted icing sugar with 2 tablespoons of lemon juice until smooth.

Breads made from Sweet Dough

It seems quite "magic" that one dough can be shaped into so many different treats. Once you feel at home with yeast doughs, experiment using other basic doughs from this book in similar ways. Eat your "goodies" the day you make them!

Basic Sweet Dough

2 tsp Surebake yeast
1 cup plus 2 Tbsp water
1 large egg
3 Tbsp lecithin granules, or butter
¼ cup sugar
1 tsp salt
¼ cup non-fat milk powder
3 cups Champion High Grade Flour

Bread Machine Instructions

Carefully measure all the ingredients into a 750g capacity bread machine, in the order specified by the manufacturer.

Set to the DOUGH cycle and start. When the cycle is complete, take out the dough and shape and bake as described below.

Handmade Bread Instructions

Measure the first seven ingredients into a large bowl with 1½ cups of the high grade flour and mix thoroughly. Cover and leave for 15 minutes or longer in a warm place.

Stir in the remaining flour to make a soft dough, adding a little extra warm water or flour if necessary to make a dough just firm enough to turn out and knead.

Knead the dough with the dough hook of an electric mixer or by hand on a lightly floured surface for 10 minutes, until the dough forms a soft ball which is not sticky and springs back when pressed gently.

Turn dough in 2–3 teaspoons of oil in the cleaned, dry bowl, cover with cling film and leave in a warm draught-free place for 30 minutes.

Knead the oiled dough lightly in the bowl for a minute, then shape as required for each recipe.

After shaping, leave to rise again in a warm, draught-free place, until risen to about one and a half times its original size, usually 30–60 minutes.

French Braid

To make a Fruit Braid about 30cm long, use half the dough. (Refrigerate the rest in a plastic bag, punching it down if it rises a lot before you use it.)

Roll the dough into an oval shape about 20cm x 30cm on a strip of baking paper. Mark into 3 equal strips, lengthwise, then cut the outer thirds into about 10 flaps (see diagram)

For a filling, mix together about $\frac{1}{2}$ cup of either Christmas Mincemeat, lemon honey, or jam, with 2 tablespoons of cake or biscuit crumbs or coconut or make this apricot filling: Heat together $\frac{1}{2}$ cup chopped dried apricots and $\frac{1}{4}$ cup orange juice until the liquid is absorbed. Add $\frac{1}{4}$ cup chopped almonds, 2 tablespoons each coconut and sugar and mix well. Cool.

Spread the cold filling evenly down the centre section of the dough. Tuck the ends in, then fold alternate strips over the filling as if you were plaiting. The plaited braid should have an even shape, so taper it in once you pass the middle. Tuck the ends of the last two pieces underneath, making the end as neat as possible.

Slide the baking paper holding the braid onto an oven tray. Leave to rise as in the basic recipe. Brush with milk or egg glaze (page 59), then bake at 200°C for about 15 minutes or until golden brown on the top and bottom. If you like, drizzle with icing (page 53) while warm, and decorate with nuts or chopped cherries.

Cream Buns

To make 12–18 cream buns: Divide once the dough into 12–18 pieces, each about 50 grams, and shape into even rolls, making sure that their tops are smooth (see page 18).

Place the shaped rolls on baking paper in a large roasting pan or other high sided pan, cover with cling film or by standing the pans in a large plastic bag, and leave to rise as described in the basic recipe.

Brush with milk or egg glaze (page 59) then bake at 200°C for 10–12 minutes or until golden brown. Cool on a rack, then cut diagonally, leaving a hinge. When cooled to room temperature, fill with a spoonful of raspberry or other jam, and plain or lightly sweetened whipped cream. Dust with icing sugar just before serving, if desired.

Fruit Buns

Make the Basic Sweet Dough, adding $\frac{1}{2}$ –1 cup of currants, sultanas, raisins, mixed fruit or a mixture of finely chopped dried apricots and other dried fruits to the dough, at the time when the bread machine beeps, or, if making by hand, when the last measure of flour is added.

Shape buns as for Cream Buns. Bake without glazing. As soon as the buns are cooked, while still very hot, brush with golden syrup glaze (page 59).

Doughnuts

To make 16–18 doughnuts: On a lightly floured surface, roll out the basic sweet dough until about 1 cm thick. Using a doughnut cutter or a round biscuit cutter, 7 cm in diameter, cut out circles, re-rolling the scraps to make more. With a 2cm cutter cut out the centre of each doughnut. (Keep these to cook at the same time as the doughnuts, since they are very popular with small children.)

Put each doughnut on a square of baking paper and leave to rise until $1\frac{1}{2}$–2 times their original size.

Heat about 5cm oil in a frypan, wok or deep frier. (It is the right heat when a scrap of dough turns golden brown in about 15 seconds.) Cook doughnuts one or two at a time, turning to cook the other side before lifting out and leaving to drain on paper towels. (The "Holes" should cook in about 45 seconds.)

Toss each drained, cool doughnut in a plastic bag with a 1–2 teaspoons cinnamon sugar (made by mixing $\frac{1}{4}$ cup castor sugar with 1 teaspoon cinnamon). These are best eaten within half an hour of cooking.

Cinnamon Swirls

The warm, inviting smell of yeast and cinnamon wafting through the house as these rolls cook is a promise of a treat to come. Reward your "team" with these delicious Cinnamon Swirls after they have finished all the jobs you wanted done.

Makes about 12 rolls:

2 tsp Surebake yeast
½ cup milk
2 Tbsp warm water
1 Tbsp sugar
1 tsp salt
25g butter, melted
2 cups Champion High Grade Flour

Filling and topping, see below

Bread Machine Instructions

Carefully measure all the ingredients into a 750g capacity bread machine, in the order specified by the manufacturer.

Set to the DOUGH cycle and START. When the dough is ready, tip it out onto a lightly floured surface and follow the instructions for shaping and baking below.

Handmade Bread Instructions

Measure the first six ingredients into a bowl with half the flour. Cover and leave to stand for 15 minutes in a warm place.

Stir in the remaining flour, with a little extra flour or water if necessary to make a dough just firm enough to knead.

Knead with the dough hook of an electric mixer or by hand on a lightly floured surface, for 10 minutes or until the dough forms a soft ball which springs back when lightly pressed.

Turn in 2 teaspoons of oil in the cleaned, dry bowl, cover with cling film and leave in a warm draught-free place for 30–40 minutes, then knead the dough lightly in the bowl for a minute.

Shaping and Baking

Rub 2 tablespoons of soft butter fairly evenly over the bottom and up the sides of a 20–23cm round cake pan, then sprinkle 2 tablespoons each of brown sugar and chopped walnuts over the bottom.

Roll the dough out evenly so it's about 30 cm square, then brush it lightly with a little melted butter. Sprinkle it with ½ cup brown sugar, 1 teaspoon of cinnamon, and 2 tablespoons of chopped walnuts if you like.

Roll up to form a cylinder, then cut this into about 8–12 fairly even slices. (Make the larger number for the larger pan.) Arrange these, cut side down, as evenly as you can in the prepared cake tin, leaving space around each roll for spreading. Cover with cling film and leave to rise in a warm draught-free place for about 60 minutes or until twice the original size.

Bake at 180°C for 20–30 minutes or until golden brown. Carefully turn the loaf out of the tin onto a plate or board straight away and serve warm.

Naan

Although we like all the Indian flat breads we have tried, Naan is our favourite. We are just as happy to eat Naan with a barbecue as we are with a curry – in fact, we like them with almost any meal.

Makes 8 Naan breads:

3 tsp Surebake yeast
¾ cup warm water plus 2 Tbsp
¼ cup plain, unsweetened yoghurt
50g butter, melted
1 tsp sugar
1 tsp salt
1 cup Champion Wholemeal Flour
2 cups Champion High Grade Flour
Extra butter or oil
sesame or cumin seed, optional

Bread Machine Instructions

Carefully measure all the ingredients into a 750g capacity bread machine, in the order specified by the manufacturer.

Set to the DOUGH cycle and START. When the dough is ready, tip out onto a lightly floured surface and follow the instructions for shaping and baking given below.

Handmade Bread Instructions

Measure the first seven ingredients into a large bowl and mix well. Cover and leave 15 minutes or longer in a warm place.

Stir in the high grade flour, adding a little extra warm water or flour if necessary to make a dough just firm enough to knead.

Knead with the dough hook of an electric mixer or by hand, on a lightly floured surface for 10 minutes. (Try to keep the dough as soft as you can since a soft dough produces good Naan) adding a little extra water if it is too firm, and as little flour as you need, if it is too soft to work with. After kneading, the dough should form a soft ball which springs back when pressed gently.

Turn dough in 2 teaspoons of oil in the cleaned, dry bowl, cover with cling film and leave in a warm draught-free place for 30 minutes, then turn out and knead lightly for about a minute.

Shaping and Baking

Divide the dough first into quarters, then halve these to give eight balls, cover and leave to stand for five minutes.

Roll each ball out into a flat egg shape about 18cm wide and 22–23cm long. Brush each side with the extra melted butter or oil. Sprinkle with sesame or cumin seeds if you like.

Heat oven to 225°C –250°C, with a heavy cast iron frypan or griddle on a shelf just below the middle. Place one bread at a time on the very hot pan, and cook for about 4 minutes (turning after 2 minutes) until puffed and lightly browned on both sides (or cook on the hot plate of your barbecue, turning once as above).

Eat soon after baking.

Shaping Bread Dough

Bread dough may be shaped in many ways to make loaves, rolls or a variety of other shapes.

In the individual recipes in this book, we have given suggestions for shaping each dough in only a few ways.

Initially, we hope that you will make a number of the breads, following our instructions precisely until you feel comfortable working with bread dough.

Once you have reached this stage we are sure that you will be ready to have fun, shaping the doughs in other ways.

We have compiled the following list, so that you can look up the shaping details on the pages listed, then use them to shape whatever dough you have made by hand or in a bread machine.

There are, however, two very wet doughs which we do not think you will be able to shape in other ways. Ciabatta, page 30 is wonderful just the way it is, and loses its character if you change it. Heavy Multigrain Bread, page 12, is too wet to knead and shape by hand, but you can add more flour, until it is firm enough to shape as you like. The resulting dough will make a lighter, more open-textured bread than the original recipe.

Shaping Guide

Rectangular tinned loaf, see page 8 and many other pages.

Muffin buns, see page 10. Make sure you spray the pans well, so they don't stick.

Monkey bread, see page 10. Monkey bread is easy to pull apart. You can make your own variations using strips of dough instead of balls. Bake in well oiled or buttered loaf tins, ring pans, or in muffin pans. Have fun!

Round loaf, see page 15. We usually put our round loaves in a large round cake tin, just in case they spread more than we want them to as the dough rises and bakes. You don't HAVE to do this, though.

Loaves with a spiral pattern through them, see page 16. Top rolled-out dough with a sweet or savoury mixture, and roll up.

Round bread rolls, see pages 18, 55

Long rolls, see page 18

Hamburger buns, see page 19

Hot dog buns, see page 19

Pizza, see page 20

Pita bread, see page 20

Breadsticks, see page 21

Pinwheels, see pages 21 and 56

Filled long loaf, see page 22

Calzone (folded pizza), see page 22

Focaccia shaping, see pages 27, 28

Crostini, see page 29

French bread shape, see page 31

Cottage loaf, see page 32

Braided loaf, see page 35

Twisted free-standing loaf, see page 36

Checker-board topped loaf, see page 38

Oval free-standing loaves, see page 39

Rolled triangles, roll dough thinly, brush with butter, and cut into triangles. Enclose a filling before rolling up, see page 44

Rolled "snails" see page 45

Soft-sided buns, see page 50

Ring, see page 53. OR snip a long filled roll part way through, at 3 cm intervals, and join the ends to form a ring. (Have the snipped part outermost.) Twist cut pieces so they lie flat on oven tray.

Filled braid, see page 54

Flat breads, see pages 20, 27, 28, 31, 57

Bread Glazes and Toppings

What you put on the surface of the bread you make affects its appearance a lot.

Floury Topped Breads

A floury top gives a "cottagy", home-baked look to a loaf or rolls. Sprinkle the flour to the risen loaf using a shaker with small holes or a sieve. If you lightly wet the surface first, the flour sticks better, and the crust tends to be firmer.

If you score the crust of the risen loaf with a very sharp blade after flouring it, before baking it, the cuts will be an attractive, contrasting colour.

Egg Glaze for Breads

If you brush the surface of the risen loaf with an egg glaze just before it is baked, it will brown better and have an attractive shine. The crust will be thin and fairly tender.

Shake together in a tightly closed jar, or beat with a fork in a bowl:

1 egg

1 Tbsp water

½ tsp sugar

This will keep in the refrigerator for 2-3 days.

For more shine, brush on extra glaze after cooking, while bread is very hot.

An egg glaze sticks a topping onto a loaf, too. Brush the uncooked bread with the glaze then sprinkle with poppy seeds, sesame seeds, sunflower or pumpkin seeds, coarse cornmeal, etc.

Note: Take care. Toppings such as kibbled grains harden during cooking. Do not break your teeth!

Milk Glazed Breads

For a slightly glazed appearance and a thin crust, brush the bread with milk instead of egg glaze. Milk containing some fat works better than very low fat milk.

Water and Steam

For a crusty loaf, put a roasting pan containing water 1cm deep on the bottom shelf of the oven five minutes before you put the bread in. For extra crustiness, spray the crust with water several times during cooking. Remove the pan of water 5 minutes before you take the bread from the oven. Spraying by itself, without the pan of water in the oven is not particularly effective.

A longer cooking time produces a crustier loaf, but you must be careful not to overcook the bread.

Golden Syrup Glaze

To give a shiny brown glaze to sweet buns and bread, make a syrup by bringing to the boil 1 tablespoon each of golden syrup, honey and water. Brush on buns and breads (which have not been egg-glazed) as soon as they come from the oven. This glaze softens the crust, too.

For a darker coloured glaze replace the honey with extra syrup. For a lighter coloured glaze, use all honey and no syrup.

Ingredients used in Breadmaking

WHOLE WHEAT is the basic raw material for all flour production. Wheat seeds, sometimes called wheat berries, consist of tough bran layers surrounding the starchy white endosperm, and at the blunt ends the yellowish embryos or germ. High in fibre, whole wheat can be soaked and used in grain breads, but is more commonly used in its kibbled form (see next page). Soak or boil before adding to dough.

WHITE FLOUR During the process of milling, the starchy white inner part (endosperm) is separated from the bran and germ, then crushed to give flour. Unfortunately this process removes a considerable amount of fibre (from the bran) and vitamins (from the bran and germ), but effectively increases the proportions of starch and protein which are essential for the manufacture of good bread.

Most retail outlets offer two types of white flour (excluding self-raising), these are High Grade Flour (sometimes called Bread Flour or Baker's Flour) and Standard Plain Flour. **HIGH GRADE** OR **BREAD FLOUR**, used for most recipes in this book, is "stronger" than Standard Plain Flour, having a higher protein content, and making it particularly suitable for use in bread. **STANDARD PLAIN FLOUR**, with a lower protein content, is more suitable for most other general baking (cakes, biscuits etc.), but is occasionally used in bread where a soft or light product is desired.

WHOLEMEAL FLOUR is literally the product produced when the whole wheat grain is crushed into flour. Wholemeal flour is much higher in fibre and some vitamins than white flour. Stoneground wholemeal flours are made this way, but large modern flour mills tend to separate the bran, germ and endosperm at an early stage, and these are then recombined, in proportions which give the wholemeal flour we know.

As wholemeal flours contain the germ which is relatively rich in oils*, they will go rancid in time. To avoid this, keep in a cool dark place and buy quantities that you can use within 4–6 weeks. If you have the space, consider storing wholemeal flour in the refrigerator or freezer, but remember to allow it to return to room temperature before use.

The presence of the bran effectively dilutes the gluten proteins present. It provides additional weight for the gluten network formed in the dough to support. For this reason, loaves made solely (or with high proportions) of wholemeal flour, will rise less and be more dense than those made with white flour. For best results we try not to use more than a 50/50 wholemeal to white flour ratio. If substituting wholemeal for white flour, remember to increase the water content by 1–2 tablespoons per cup of wholemeal used, as the bran also absorbs more water. It may also be worth adding 1–2 teaspoons of gluten per cup of wholemeal used.

* Stonegrinding distributes these oils differently in the flour. This can affect baking quality and some bread machine makers suggest avoiding its use.

ORGANIC FLOUR Organic flour is obtainable, but may vary in bread-making quality. The amount of organic wheat grown is not large, so millers may not be as selective with the raw material as they are with conventionally farmed wheat.

GLUTEN OR GLUTEN FLOUR Gluten (sometimes called Vital Wheat Gluten) is a collective term for the dough forming proteins of wheat. It is the gluten that gives bread dough its "strength" and most importantly, elasticity. (The ability to form an elastic dough is unique to wheat.)

The gluten flour we buy is prepared by washing the starch out of dough, then drying and grinding the sticky mass of protein left behind.

To an extent, adding additional gluten to a dough will increase the size of loaves (particularly true for those with high proportions of wholemeal or whole grains). However, adding gluten also increases the amount of work that must be put into dough to produce good bread, and this translates into longer kneading or mixing times. As bread machines mix for fixed periods of time,

Ingredients used in Breadmaking

if there is too much gluten present the dough will not "fully develop" in the time allowed, and there may be no improvement in the finished loaf.

WHEATGERM is the embryo of the wheat seed. If the seed is allowed to sprout it is the germ which will grow into the new plant, drawing food from the starchy endosperm. Although high in non-gluten proteins, oils, B vitamins, vitamin E and minerals, unfortunately wheatgerm does little for baking quality. However, adding 1–2 tablespoons per loaf will boost the nutritive value of your bread without affecting quality too much.

BRAN (WHEATBRAN) is the protective outer layers of the wheat grain which are removed during the milling of white flour. A very good source of fibre and relatively high in vitamins and minerals, but containing no gluten forming proteins. Best added sparingly (1–2 tablespoons per loaf) as the additional weight (for the gluten to hold) will decrease the size of loaves. Add a little extra additional water when adding extra bran to bread.

BUCKWHEAT FLOUR Buckwheat is not true wheat at all and contains no gluten. Add sparingly to bread for its nutty flavour.

SOYA FLOUR is flour made from ground soya beans. It is a good source of additional proteins, complementing those in wheat. It may be added in small quantities but if you add too much you will get a distinctive "beany" flavour.

RYE MEAL (RYE MEAL FLOUR) is a fine floury meal produced by grinding whole rye grains. Rye does contain some gluten protein but not as much as wheat. Rye meal may be used in place of some wheat flour (don't replace more than a third) but you will tend to get a denser, more solid loaf.

RYE FLOUR is produced from the starchy endosperm of the rye grain in much the same way as white flour. It may vary from quite light in colour to quite dark, depending on the extraction rate (how hard the bran is scraped) during milling. It may be used to replace wheat flour in part, and is very common in northern European bread.

CORN MEAL may vary in size from a fine yellow powder to coarse yellow chunks. It contains no gluten, so will not form a dough as wheat flour does. Add in small proportions for texture and/or visual appeal.

KIBBLED WHEAT is coarsely chopped wheat grains, a good source of fibre and texture. It should be soaked or boiled before adding to the dough. Bulgar (burghul) is kibbled wheat which has been cooked and dried. In theory it can be added to bread dough unsoaked (but add more water as well).

KIBBLED RYE is coarsely chopped whole rye grains added to bread for flavour texture and additional fibre. It should be soaked or boiled before use in bread.

KIBBLE MIX (CEREAL MIX) is a pre-prepared mixture of kibbled grains, used by bakeries. Not usually available from supermarkets, it may be obtained from flour mills. It often looks more interesting than standard kibbled grains, as the mill may add coloured (purple) wheat which is a specialty of New Zealand.

ROLLED OATS are whole oats that have been steamed then rolled flat. Add in small quantities for flavour, texture and added fibre. Rolled oats hold water, so bread made with them stales more slowly.

LECITHIN GRANULES A natural emulsifier produced from soya beans. Emulsifiers improve the consistency and performance of doughs as well as slowing the staling of bread. Lecithin granules may be used in place of non-emulsifying fats like oil or butter in most recipes, and have the additional advantage of being lower in calories on a volume for volume basis.

YEAST We have used two types of yeast in this book, Active Dried Yeast and Surebake Yeast. Active Dried Yeast is an all-purpose yeast which may be used for processes other than bread making e.g. brewing. Surebake yeast has been formulated especially for bread making, and in most situations, produces better bread.

Remember that yeast is a living organism, and should be kept in the refrigerator. High temperatures used too early in the bread-making process will kill the yeast so the bread will not rise. On the other hand if the dough is too cool, the bread will rise very slowly. (Occasionally this is desirable).

61

Weights and Measures

When you make bread by hand, exact flour and liquid measurements are not as important as they are in much other baking, since you work by feel, adding extra flour as it is needed. The exact amount you use may differ with each batch of flour you buy.

When you make bread in a bread machine it is much more important to measure accurately, then to adjust the wetness or dryness of the dough as the machine kneads it (see page 4).

Take care when measuring yeast, salt and sugar, since small amounts of these may affect your dough considerably.

Use level metric 250ml cups and metric measuring spoons unless the recipe specifies otherwise. 1 tablespoon measures 15ml, and 1 teaspoon 5 ml. For ease and speed we use single capacity measuring cups for quarter and half cup quantities.

When measuring liquids, fill the containers brimming full.

Small amounts of butter are measured by volume. 1 teaspoon weighs 5 grams and 1 tablespoon weighs about 15 grams.

When we measured our flour, we stirred the flour near the top of our storage container, then scooped it lightly into the measuring cup without packing, tapping or shaking the cup, and levelled the top. 1 cup of bread/high quality/bakers flour weighs 135–140g when measured like this.

It is easy, even for experienced cooks, to leave out an ingredient every now and then. Leaving out (or doubling up on) yeast, salt or sugar can ruin your bread, so take extra care! We find it best to line up all the ingredients in the recipe, check that this line-up is complete, then measure each ingredient into our bowl, putting the container aside (somewhere different) after we have done this. Then, before we go on to the next step, we check to make sure we have not left melted butter or warmed liquid in our microwave oven!

ACKNOWLEDGEMENTS

We would like to thank the firms who provided us with the following foods and products: • ALISON'S CHOICE Dried fruit, nuts, seeds etc • ALISON'S MICROWAVE DISHES Lamnei Plastics • APRICOT GLAZE Barkers Food Processors Ltd • BEER Emerson's Breweries • CANNED TOMATO PRODUCTS ETC J.Wattie Foods • CHEESE Ferndale, Mainland • CHEF MATE S.C. Johnson & Son • DRIED HERBS AND SPICES Empire Foodstuffs • FRESH EGGS Bennicks Poultry Farm, Buller Rd, Levin • KIBBLED GRAINS Champion Flour Mills • LUPI OLIVE OIL & BALSAMIC VINEGAR William Aitken & Co. • PESTO Genoese Foods • SMOKED SALMON Southern Ocean Seafoods • BREAD MACHINE Sunbeam • TARARUA PRODUCTS Tui Foods • TEFLON LINERS Surebrand, Auckland. EDMONDS SUREBAKE AND EDMONDS ACTIVE DRY YEAST, CHAMPION HIGH GRADE, STANDARD AND WHOLEMEAL FLOURS Bluebird Foods Ltd.

The wonderful range of tablewear in the photographs was supplied by the following: • Page 14 Basket & Board - The Homestore: Napkin - Levene & Co Ltd • Page 23 Round board and glass - Levene & Co Ltd • Page 41 Cup, saucer, spoon, napkin ring, spreader - The Homestore: Bread basket - Levene & Co Ltd • Page 42 Tray, mug, plate & napkin - Levene & Co Ltd: Bowl - Andrew Hawley • Page 51 Plate & basket - Levene: Rooster - Andrew Hawley • Page 52 Platter, napkin, cup, saucer & plate - Levene & Co Ltd: Napkin ring & teaspoon - The Homestore

WE USED THE FOLLOWING: Panasonic, Perfect Baker, Sunbeam, and Toshiba bread machines and a Kenwood Chef mixer.

Index

CONVERSIONS FOR 500G MACHINES

Most bread machines for sale at present make a 750g (1½ lb) or larger loaf, using 3 or more cups of flour. However some older (and at least one new) bread machines are designed to make a 500g (1lb) loaf using about 2 cups flour. If you have one of these machines, do not overload it, but simply use two thirds of the quantities given in our recipes. The table below gives approximately scaled down quantities of our commonly used measures.

750g Machines	500g Machines
1 tsp	scant ¾ tsp
2 tsp	1½ tsp
3 tsp	2 tsp
1 Tbsp	2 tsp
2 Tbsp	1 Tbsp plus 1 tsp
3 Tbsp	2 Tbsp
¼ cup	2 Tbsp plus 2 tsp
½ cup	¼ cup plus 1 Tbsp
¾ cup	½ cup
1 cup	½ cup plus 2 Tbsp
1¼ cups	¾ cup plus 1 Tbsp
1½ cups	1 cup
2 cups	1¼ cups plus 1 Tbsp
2½ cups	1½ cups plus 3 Tbsp
3 cups	2 cups
1 large egg	1 small egg

Remember to check the dough after a few minutes of mixing. It should have formed a smooth-looking ball or cylinder. If it is too wet, add 1 tablespoon of flour, if too dry add 2 teaspoons water. Repeat until the dough is the right consistency.

Knives by Mail Order

I use and wholeheartedly recommend these high quality Swiss knives.

All knives have black dishwasher-proof handles and come in either a plastic sheath or a box.

VEGETABLE KNIFE - $8.00 Pointed, straight edged, 85mm blade, in a plastic sheath. For peeling vegetables and cutting small objects.

UTILITY KNIFE - $9.50 Pointed 103mm blade. For boning chicken and meat and general kitchen use.

SERRATED KNIFE - $9.50 Rounded end, 110mm serrated blade. Never needs sharpening. For slicing (even very fresh) bread and baking, tomatoes and fruit, etc.

THREE PIECE SET - $22.00 Serrated knife (as above), 85mm blade vegetable knife with pointed tip, and (right-handed) potato peeler.

GIFT BOX KNIFE SET - $44.00 Five knives and potato peeler. Contains the three pieces in the set above plus straight bladed vegetable knife, blade 85mm; serrated edged vegetable knife, blade 85mm; and small serrated utility 85mm.

SERRATED CARVING KNIFE - $28.50 Cutting edge 21 cm, overall length 33 cm. Never requires sharpening. Excellent for bread.

STEEL - $20.00 20 cm blade, 34 cm total length.

All prices include GST. Prices current at time of publishing, subject to change without notice. Please add $3.50 post & packing to all orders (any number of items).

Make cheques payable to Alison Holst Mail Orders and post to: Alison Holst Mail Orders

>Freepost 124807
>P.O.Box 17-016
>Wellington.

Or, visit us at www.holst.co.nz